I0427472

THIS BOOK

BELONGS TO

....

....

Copyright @2023

All rights reserved. No part of this publication may be reproduced, stored in a retrieval system, or transmitted in any form or by any means, electronic, mechanical, photocopying, recording or otherwise, without the prior written permission of the Publisher.

Author's Afterthoughts

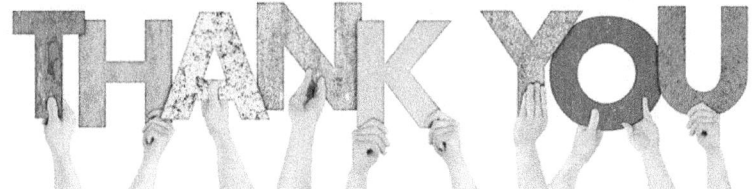

With so many books out there to choose from, I want to thank you for choosing this one and taking precious time out of your life to buy and read my work. Readers like you are the reason I take such passion in creating these books.

It is with gratitude and humility that I express how honored I am to become a part of your life and I hope that you take the same pleasure in reading this book as I did in writing it.

Can I ask one small favour? I ask that you write an honest and open review on Amazon of what you thought of the book. This will help other readers make an informed choice on whether to buy this book.

My sincerest thanks.

Table of Contents

SUMMARY

Raccoons have long been a subject of fascination for many people. These small, masked creatures have captured the attention and curiosity of both children and adults alike. From their unique physical features to their clever and resourceful behavior, raccoons have become a beloved and intriguing animal species.

One of the reasons for the fascination with raccoons is their distinctive appearance. With their black fur, white facial markings, and bushy tails, raccoons have a striking and memorable look. Their mask-like facial markings have often been associated with mischief and cunning, adding to their allure. Additionally, their nimble paws and dexterous fingers make them appear almost human-like, further captivating our interest.

Another aspect that contributes to the fascination with raccoons is their adaptability and intelligence. Raccoons are highly adaptable creatures, able to thrive in a variety of environments, from forests to urban areas. They have a remarkable ability to problem-solve and are known for their resourcefulness. Raccoons have been observed using their paws to manipulate objects and even open containers, showcasing their cleverness and ingenuity.

Furthermore, raccoons exhibit a wide range of behaviors that captivate our attention. They are known for their nocturnal habits, often seen scavenging for food under the cover of darkness. Raccoons are omnivorous, meaning they eat both plants and animals, which adds to their versatility and adaptability. Their foraging behavior, as well as their ability to climb trees and swim, make them fascinating to observe in their natural habitats.

Raccoons also have a mischievous and playful nature, which adds to their charm. They are known for their curiosity and have been observed exploring their surroundings with great enthusiasm. This playful behavior, combined with their cleverness, has led to numerous stories and anecdotes about raccoons outsmarting humans or getting into mischief.

In addition to their physical and behavioral characteristics, raccoons have also become popular in popular culture. They have been featured in various forms of media, including cartoons, movies, and even as mascots for sports teams. This exposure has further contributed to the fascination with raccoons, as they have become iconic and recognizable symbols in many societies.

Overall, the fascination with raccoons stems from their unique physical features, adaptability, intelligence, playful behavior, and their presence in popular culture. These factors combine to make raccoons a captivating and beloved animal species that continues to intrigue and delight people

Basic sketching techniques are fundamental skills that every artist should master. Sketching is the process of quickly capturing ideas and concepts on paper using simple lines and shapes. It is a versatile and essential skill that can be applied to various art forms, such as drawing, painting, and even digital art.

One of the most important aspects of sketching is observation. Artists must train their eyes to see and understand the world around them. This involves studying the proportions, shapes, and details of objects and scenes. By observing and analyzing the subject matter, artists can accurately represent it on paper.

Another crucial technique in sketching is contour drawing. Contour drawing involves drawing the outline or contour of an object without lifting the pencil from the paper. This technique helps artists understand the form and structure of the subject. It also helps in capturing the overall shape and proportions accurately.

Shading is another essential technique in sketching. It involves adding value and depth to the sketch by using different tones and gradients. Shading helps create a three-dimensional effect and adds realism to the drawing. Artists can achieve shading by using various techniques, such as hatching, cross-hatching, and blending.

Understanding perspective is also crucial in sketching. Perspective refers to the way objects appear in relation to each other and the viewer. It helps create a sense of depth and distance in the drawing. Artists must learn the principles of one-point, two-point, and three-point perspective to accurately represent objects in their sketches.

Sketching also involves the use of different drawing tools. Pencils, charcoal, and ink pens are commonly used for sketching. Each tool has its own unique qualities and effects, allowing artists to experiment and create different textures and styles.

Lastly, practice is key to improving sketching skills. Artists should dedicate regular time to sketching and experimenting with different techniques. By practicing regularly, artists can refine their skills, develop their own style, and gain confidence in their abilities.

In conclusion, basic sketching techniques are essential for any artist. By mastering observation, contour drawing, shading, perspective, and using different drawing tools, artists can create accurate and expressive sketches. With practice and dedication, artists can continue to develop their skills and create stunning works of art.

Studying raccoon anatomy involves a comprehensive examination of the physical structure and internal systems of these fascinating creatures. Raccoons, scientifically known as Procyon lotor, are medium-sized mammals native to North America. They are known for their distinctive black mask-like markings around their eyes and their ringed tails.

To begin studying raccoon anatomy, one must first explore their external features. Raccoons have a robust and compact body, typically measuring around 16 to 28 inches in length, excluding their tail. Their fur is dense and varies in color, ranging from grayish-brown to reddish-brown. The fur on their underbelly is usually lighter in color. Raccoons have sharp claws on their front paws, which they use for climbing trees and manipulating objects. Their hind legs are longer and more muscular, enabling them to run and jump with agility.

Moving on to their head, raccoons possess a distinct facial structure. Their most recognizable feature is the black mask-like markings around their eyes, which extend to their cheeks. These markings serve as a form of camouflage and may also help reduce glare. Raccoons have a pointed snout and a small, rounded pair of ears. Their ears are highly sensitive and can rotate independently, allowing them to detect sounds from various directions.

Delving deeper into raccoon anatomy, it is essential to examine their internal systems. Like other mammals, raccoons have a complex skeletal structure that provides support and protection. Their skeleton consists of bones, joints, and cartilage. The raccoon's skull is relatively small and elongated, housing their brain and sensory organs. Their teeth are sharp and well-suited for their omnivorous diet, which includes both plant matter and small animals.

Raccoons possess a highly adaptable digestive system. Their teeth are designed to tear and crush food, while their stomachs have the ability to digest a wide range of food types. This adaptability allows raccoons to thrive in various habitats and consume a diverse diet, including fruits, nuts, insects, small mammals, and even garbage.

The circulatory system of raccoons is responsible for transporting oxygen, nutrients, and waste products throughout their bodies. Their heart pumps blood through a network of blood vessels, ensuring the delivery of essential substances to different organs and tissues. Raccoons also have a respiratory system that enables them to breathe efficiently.

Analyzing Raccoon Postures and Expressions is a fascinating field of study that involves observing and interpreting the various physical positions and facial expressions exhibited by raccoons. Raccoons are highly intelligent and adaptable creatures, known for their dexterous paws and mischievous nature. By closely examining their postures and expressions, researchers and animal behaviorists can gain valuable insights into their emotions, intentions, and overall well-being.

One aspect of raccoon postures that is often analyzed is their body positioning. Raccoons have a wide range of postures, each conveying a different message. For example, an upright and alert posture indicates a state of vigilance and readiness, suggesting that the raccoon is on high alert and potentially preparing for a threat. On the other hand, a relaxed and sprawled-out posture suggests a sense of comfort and security, indicating that the raccoon feels safe in its environment.

Facial expressions also play a crucial role in understanding raccoon behavior. Raccoons have expressive faces, with a wide range of movements and gestures that can convey various emotions. For instance, a raccoon with raised eyebrows and wide eyes may be expressing surprise or fear, while narrowed eyes and a wrinkled nose could indicate aggression or annoyance. By carefully observing these facial expressions, researchers can gain insights into the raccoon's emotional state and potentially predict its next actions.

Analyzing raccoon postures and expressions can also provide valuable information about their social interactions and communication. Raccoons are known to be highly social animals, and they use a combination of body language and vocalizations to communicate with each other. By studying their postures and expressions during social interactions, researchers can decipher the subtle cues and signals that raccoons use to convey dominance, submission, or even playfulness. This knowledge can help us better understand raccoon social dynamics and how they form and maintain relationships within their groups.

Furthermore, analyzing raccoon postures and expressions can have practical applications in wildlife conservation and management. By understanding the body language and facial expressions of raccoons, researchers can develop non-invasive methods to assess their stress levels and overall well-being in captivity or in the wild. This information can be used to improve their living conditions, identify potential health issues, and develop strategies for their conservation and protection.

In conclusion, analyzing raccoon postures and expressions is a fascinating and important field of study that provides valuable insights into their emotions, intentions, social interactions, and overall well-being. By closely

The playful raccoon is seen in action, showcasing its agile and mischievous nature. With its nimble movements and quick reflexes, it effortlessly climbs trees, jumps from branch to branch, and scurries across the ground. Its sleek and dexterous paws allow it to manipulate objects with ease, making it a master at opening lids, rummaging through trash cans, and even stealing food from unsuspecting humans.

In its playful state, the raccoon engages in various activities that demonstrate its intelligence and curiosity. It is often seen rolling and tumbling around, seemingly enjoying its own company. Its sharp eyes are constantly scanning the surroundings, always on the lookout for new adventures and opportunities to satisfy its insatiable curiosity.

One of the raccoon's most notable traits is its ability to adapt to different environments. Whether it's exploring urban areas or venturing into the depths of forests, this adaptable creature effortlessly navigates its surroundings. Its keen sense of smell helps it locate food sources, while its sharp claws and teeth aid in foraging and hunting.

When it comes to social interactions, the playful raccoon is known for its gregarious nature. It often forms small groups or families, consisting of a mother and her young ones. These groups engage in playful wrestling matches, chasing each other, and engaging in friendly competitions. Through these interactions, the raccoon not only strengthens its bonds with its family members but also hones its physical and cognitive skills.

Despite its mischievous reputation, the playful raccoon also displays a gentle and affectionate side. It is not uncommon to witness raccoons grooming each other, showing care and affection towards their companions. This behavior not only helps maintain their fur's cleanliness but also strengthens the social bonds within their group.

In conclusion, the playful raccoon is a fascinating creature that captivates observers with its agile movements, mischievous antics, and adaptable nature. Its intelligence, curiosity, and social interactions make it a truly remarkable animal to observe in action.

To create a scene with multiple raccoons, one must carefully consider the setting, the behavior of the raccoons, and the overall atmosphere of the scene. The first step is to choose an appropriate location for the scene. Raccoons are typically found in wooded areas, so a forest or a park with dense vegetation would be ideal. This will provide the raccoons with a natural habitat and allow them to exhibit their natural behaviors.

Once the location is determined, it is important to understand the behavior of raccoons in order to accurately depict them in the scene. Raccoons are known for their curious and mischievous nature. They are highly intelligent animals and are often seen exploring their surroundings, searching for food, or playing with objects they find. Incorporating these behaviors into the scene will add authenticity and interest.

To create a visually appealing scene, it is important to consider the composition and arrangement of the raccoons. Placing them in different positions and poses will add depth and variety to the scene. Some raccoons could be climbing trees, while others could be foraging on the ground or interacting with each other. This will create a dynamic and lively atmosphere.

In addition to the raccoons themselves, it is important to consider the surrounding elements of the scene. Adding details such as fallen leaves, rocks, or a stream will enhance the realism of the environment. These elements can also provide opportunities for the raccoons to interact with their surroundings, such as using rocks to crack open nuts or playing in the water.

To further enhance the scene, one can also consider the lighting and time of day. Raccoons are primarily nocturnal animals, so incorporating a moonlit or starry night sky can add a sense of mystery and intrigue. The use of shadows and highlights can also create depth and add visual interest to the scene.

Overall, creating a scene with multiple raccoons requires careful attention to detail and an understanding of their behavior and natural habitat. By considering the location, behavior, composition, and surrounding elements, one can create a captivating and realistic scene that showcases the charm and playfulness of these fascinating creatures.

Incorporating natural elements such as trees, bushes, and other greenery into our surroundings has numerous benefits that extend beyond just aesthetic appeal. These elements have the power to transform any space, whether it be a residential backyard, a commercial building, or a public park, into a vibrant and inviting environment.

One of the key advantages of incorporating natural elements is the positive impact they have on our mental and physical well-being. Research has shown that being in the presence of nature can reduce stress levels, improve mood, and enhance cognitive function. The sight of trees and plants has a calming effect on our minds, helping us to relax and unwind. Additionally, spending time in green spaces has been linked to increased physical activity, which in turn promotes better overall health.

Furthermore, natural elements play a crucial role in improving air quality. Trees, for instance, act as natural air filters by absorbing carbon dioxide and releasing oxygen through the process of photosynthesis. They also help to reduce air pollution by trapping harmful particles and pollutants on their leaves and bark. By incorporating more trees and plants into our surroundings, we can create cleaner and healthier environments for ourselves and future generations.

Incorporating natural elements also contributes to the preservation of biodiversity. By providing habitats for various species of birds, insects, and other wildlife, we can help maintain a balanced ecosystem. This is particularly important in urban areas where green spaces are limited. By creating pockets of nature within our cities, we can support the survival of different species and promote biodiversity conservation.

In addition to the environmental and health benefits, incorporating natural elements can also enhance the overall beauty and appeal of any space. Trees and bushes provide shade and privacy, creating a more comfortable and enjoyable outdoor environment. They can also act as natural sound barriers, reducing noise pollution and creating a peaceful atmosphere. Moreover, the presence of greenery has been shown to increase property values and attract more visitors to public spaces, making them more vibrant and economically viable.

In conclusion, incorporating natural elements into our surroundings is not just about adding beauty and visual appeal. It has far-reaching benefits for our mental and physical well-being, as well as for the environment. By embracing nature and integrating trees, bushes, and other greenery into our spaces, we can create healthier, more sustainable, and more inviting environments for ourselves and future generations to enjoy.

Raccoons are highly adaptable creatures that can be found in a variety of natural settings across North America. These intelligent mammals are known for their distinctive black mask and ringed tail, and they are often associated with wooded areas and water sources.

One of the most common natural settings for raccoons is forests. Raccoons are excellent climbers and are well-suited to living in trees. They can make their dens in tree hollows, using branches and leaves to create a cozy and secure home. Forests provide raccoons with ample food sources, including nuts, berries, and insects. They are also skilled at foraging for small animals, such as frogs and mice, which are abundant in forested areas.

Wetlands and marshes are another natural setting where raccoons thrive. These areas offer a rich and diverse ecosystem, with plenty of food and water sources. Raccoons are excellent swimmers and are often seen wading in shallow water or hunting for fish and crayfish. Wetlands also provide raccoons with an abundance of vegetation, such as cattails and water lilies, which they can use for shelter and nesting.

Urban and suburban areas have also become natural settings for raccoons. These adaptable creatures have learned to coexist with humans and have taken advantage of the resources available in urban environments. Raccoons can be found in parks, gardens, and even residential neighborhoods, where they scavenge for food in garbage cans and dumpsters. They are known for their dexterity and problem-solving skills, which allow them to access food sources that may be hidden or protected.

Overall, raccoons are highly versatile animals that can thrive in a variety of natural settings. Whether it's in forests, wetlands, or urban areas, raccoons have adapted to make the most of their surroundings and find the resources they need to survive. Their ability to adapt and their intelligence make them a fascinating species to observe in their natural habitats.

Creating unique raccoon characters involves a combination of imagination, research, and attention to detail. Raccoons are fascinating creatures known for their mischievous nature and distinctive physical features, making them an excellent choice for character development.

To begin, it is essential to have a clear understanding of raccoon behavior and characteristics. Researching their natural habitat, diet, and social interactions can provide valuable insights into their personality traits and mannerisms. This knowledge will help in creating authentic and believable raccoon characters.

Next, it is important to consider the individuality of each raccoon character. Just like humans, raccoons have unique personalities and quirks. Some may be more adventurous and outgoing, while others may be shy and cautious. Developing a backstory for each character can help in understanding their motivations and shaping their behavior.

When designing the physical appearance of the raccoon characters, attention to detail is crucial. Raccoons are known for their distinctive black mask-like markings around their eyes and their ringed tails. Incorporating these features into the character design will make them instantly recognizable as raccoons. Additionally, considering variations in fur color and patterns can add further uniqueness to each character.

Furthermore, giving raccoon characters distinct traits and abilities can make them even more memorable. For example, one character could be exceptionally skilled at climbing trees, while another may have a knack for solving puzzles. These traits can be based on the natural abilities of raccoons, such as their agility and problem-solving skills.

To make the raccoon characters truly unique, it is important to think outside the box. Consider incorporating unexpected elements into their personalities or backgrounds. Perhaps one character has a secret talent for playing the piano or has a fascination with astronomy. These unexpected traits can add depth and complexity to the characters, making them more relatable and interesting to audiences.

In conclusion, creating unique raccoon characters requires a combination of research, imagination, and attention to detail. By understanding raccoon behavior, developing individual personalities, and incorporating distinctive physical features, these characters can come to life. Additionally, adding unexpected traits and abilities can make them even more memorable. With careful consideration and creativity, raccoon characters can captivate audiences and become beloved additions to any story or artwork.

Creating a portfolio of raccoon drawings involves a series of steps that require careful planning, creativity, and attention to detail. This process allows artists to showcase their skills and unique style while capturing the essence of these fascinating creatures.

Firstly, it is essential to gather reference materials to ensure accuracy and authenticity in the drawings. This can include photographs, videos, or even observing raccoons in their natural habitat. By studying their anatomy, behavior, and distinctive features, artists can create more realistic and engaging illustrations.

Next, artists need to decide on the medium they will use for their raccoon drawings. This can range from traditional mediums such as pencil, charcoal, or ink, to digital tools like graphic tablets or software.

Each medium offers its own set of advantages and challenges, so artists should choose the one that best suits their style and preferences.

Once the medium is chosen, artists can begin sketching their raccoon drawings. Starting with rough outlines and basic shapes, they gradually refine the details and add depth and texture to bring the raccoons to life. This stage requires patience and attention to detail, as artists strive to capture the unique characteristics of each raccoon.

After completing the initial sketches, artists can move on to adding color and shading to their raccoon drawings. This step allows for further expression and creativity, as artists can experiment with different color palettes and techniques to enhance the overall visual impact. Whether opting for a realistic or stylized approach, artists should aim to create a sense of depth and dimension in their drawings.

Once the raccoon drawings are complete, artists can consider the presentation of their portfolio. This involves selecting the best pieces to showcase, arranging them in a visually appealing manner, and considering the overall theme or narrative that ties the collection together. Artists may also choose to include additional elements such as artist statements, descriptions of the creative process, or background information on raccoons to provide a more comprehensive experience for viewers.

Finally, artists can consider various platforms to showcase their raccoon drawings. This can include physical portfolios for exhibitions or art shows, online platforms such as websites or social media, or even collaborations with galleries or art agents. By strategically promoting their work, artists can reach a wider audience and potentially attract opportunities for commissions or collaborations.

In conclusion, creating a portfolio of raccoon drawings is a meticulous and rewarding process that allows artists to showcase their skills and creativity. By carefully planning and executing each step, artists can capture the essence of these captivating creatures and present their work in

Introduction

Becoming a great artist requires creativity, patience and practice. These habits can flourish in children when they start to develop them at a young age. We believe our guide will teach your child the discipline and patience required to not just learn to draw well, but to use those qualities in everything they do. Your job as a parent is to work with your child and encourage them when stuck and feel like giving up.

The world of art is an amazing way for you and your child to communicate and bond. When you open this book and start to create with your little one, you will delight in the things you learn about them and they will feel closer to you. Your support and gentle suggestions will help them be more patient with themselves and soon they will take the time needed to create spectacular drawings of which you can both be proud.

This guide is useful for parents as it teaches fundamentals of drawing and simple techniques. By following this book with your child, adults will learn patience and develop their skills as a child's most important teacher. By spending a few hours together you will develop a strong connection and learn the best ways of communicating with each other. It is truly a rewarding experience when you and your child create a masterpiece by working together!

How to draw Racoon1

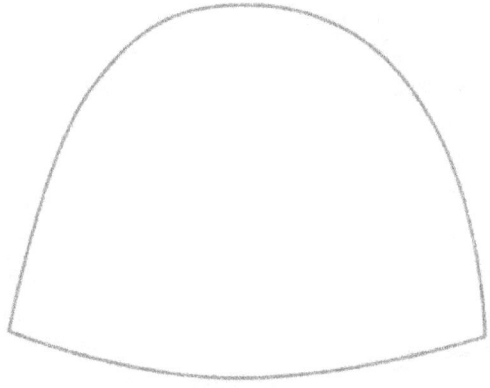

1) Draw a large head in the center of the sheet, as shown in the example.

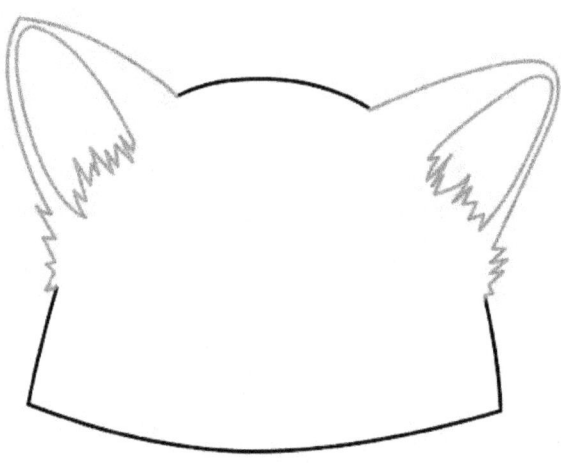

2) Draw the ears on the head, be close to the original.

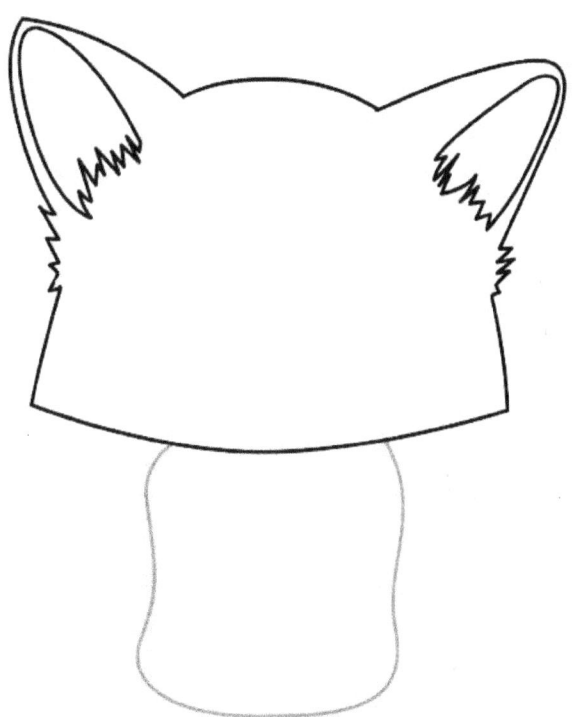

3) Get a small body under the head.

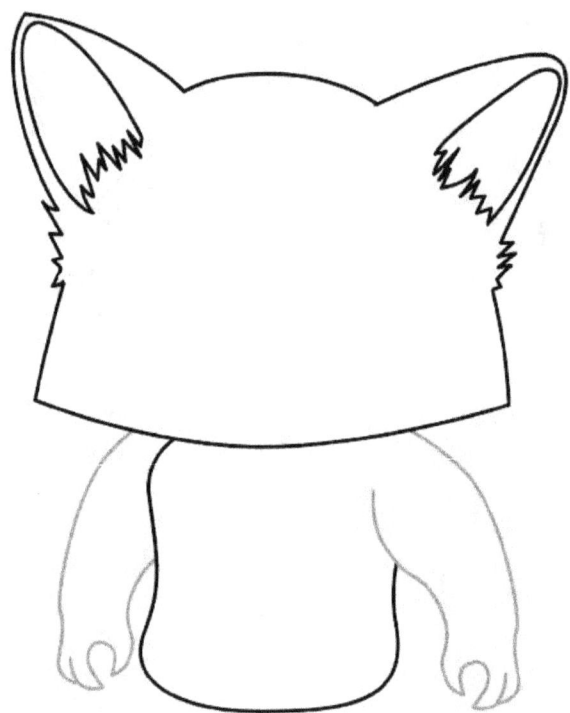

4) Draw two hands on the right and left side.

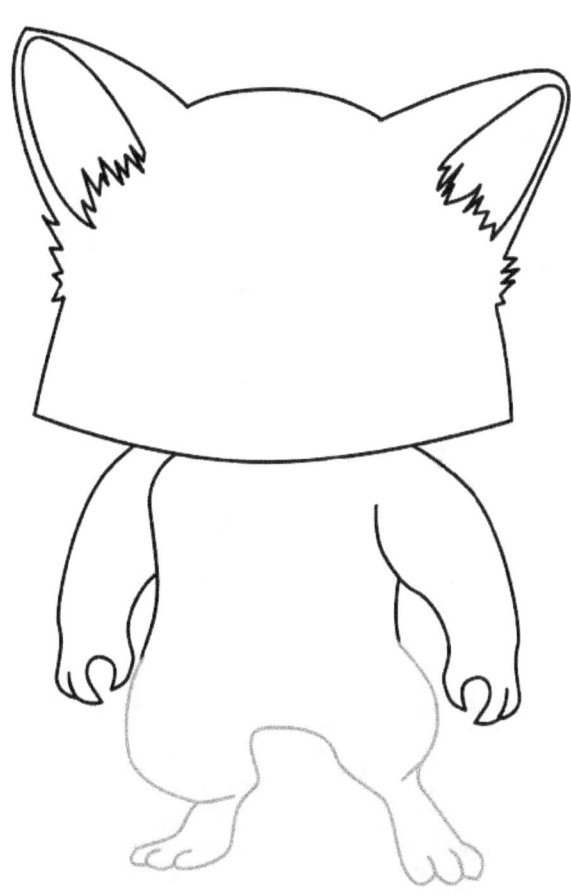

5) Draw two short legs.

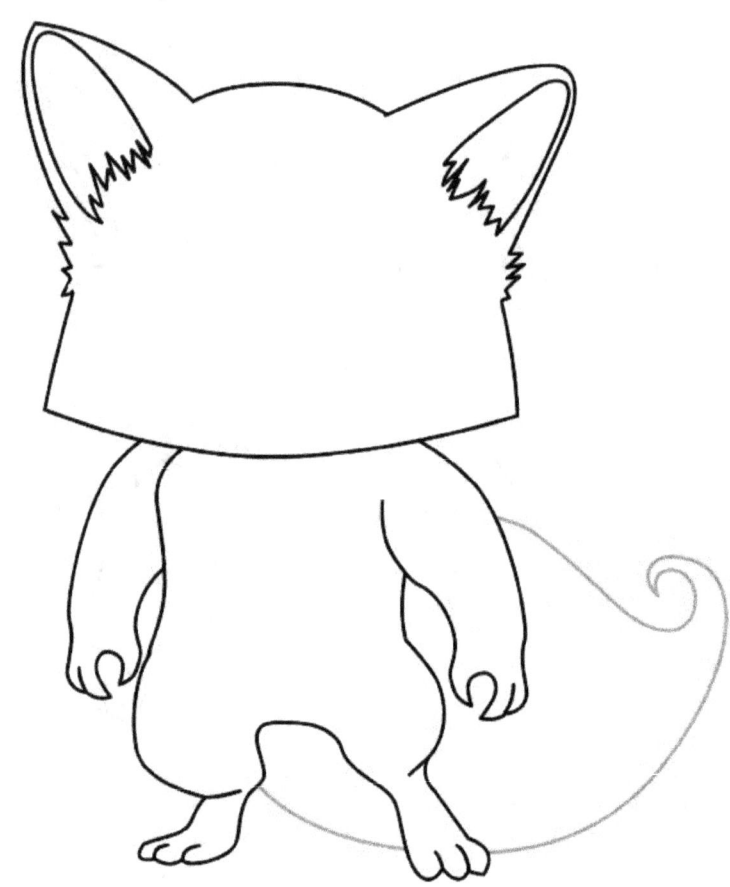

6) Draw a big fluffy tail behind the figure.

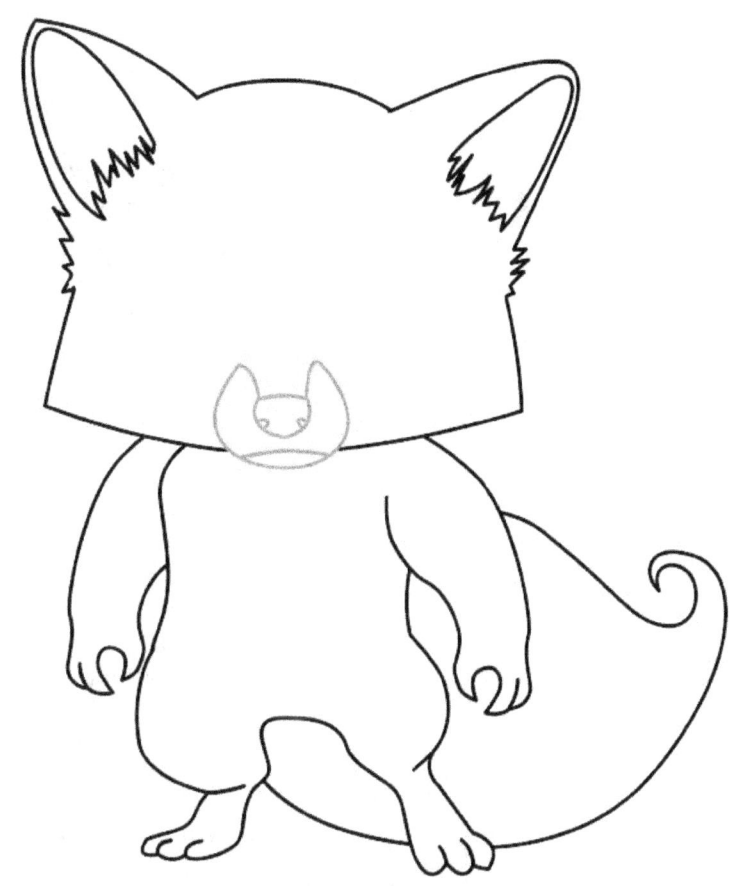

7) Add nose and mouth to face as shown in the example.

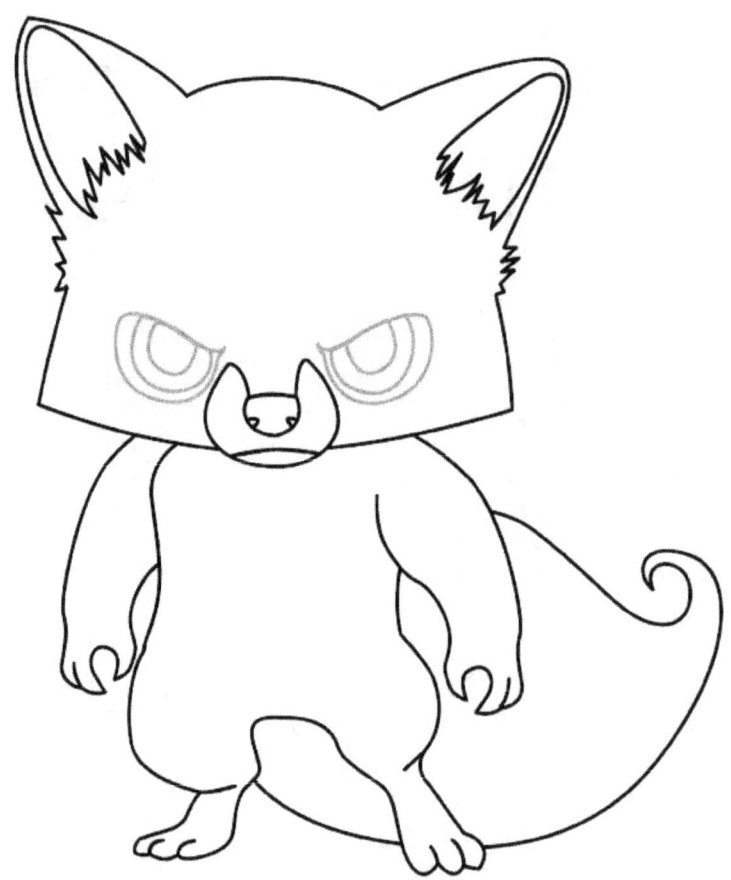

8) Draw on the head with large round eyes.

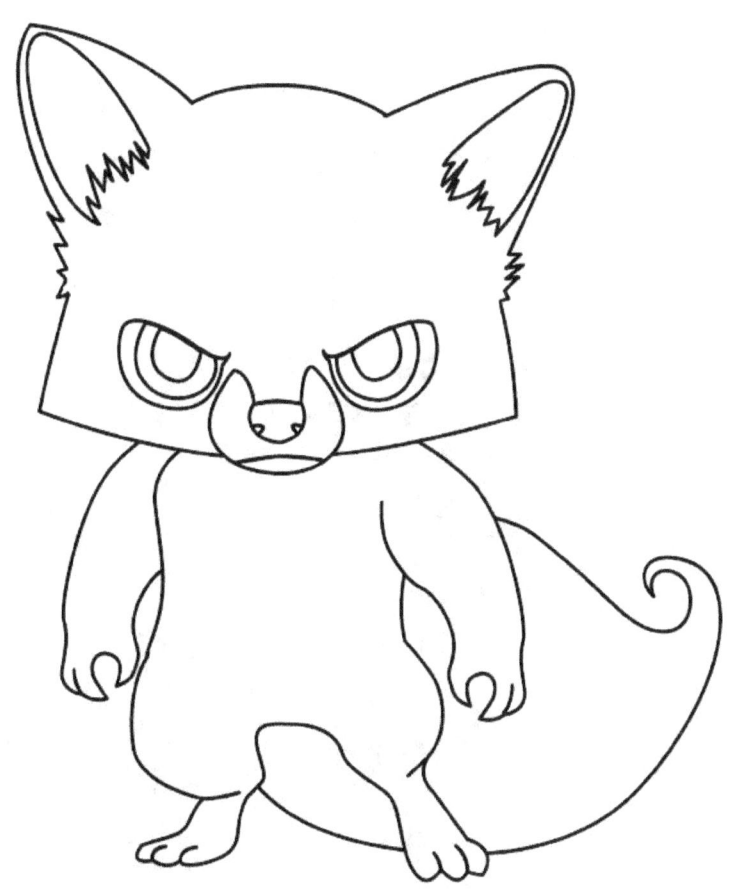

9) Done, let's start coloring!

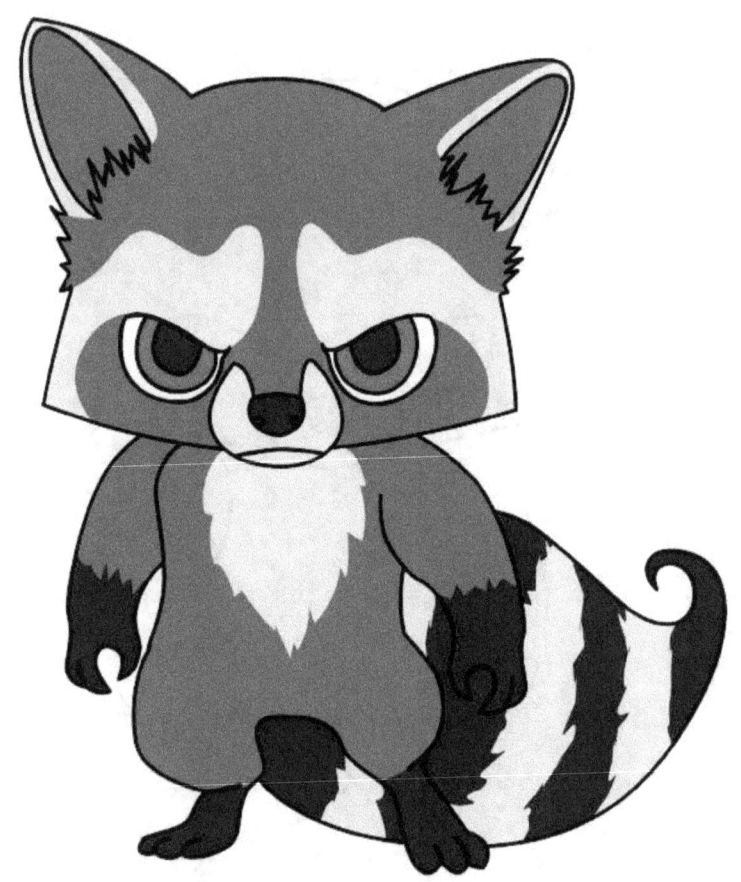

10) Color picture using grey, black and white for fur.

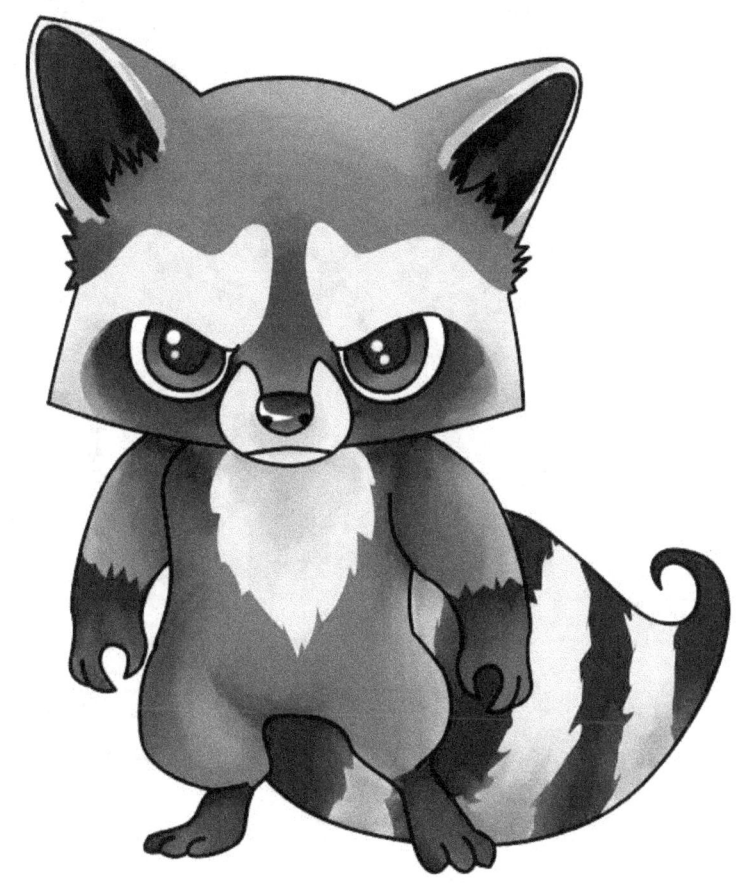

11) Add some shadows and highlights to add volume.

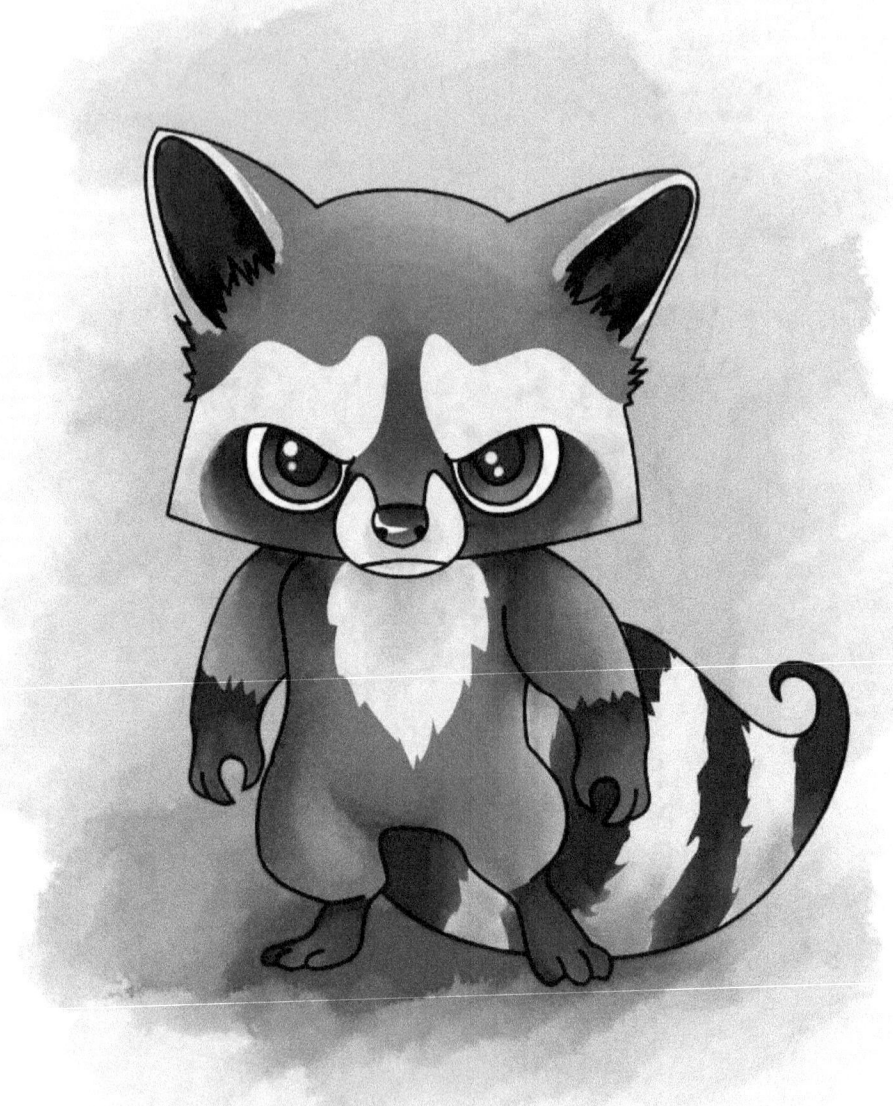

12) Colored version.

How to draw Racoon2

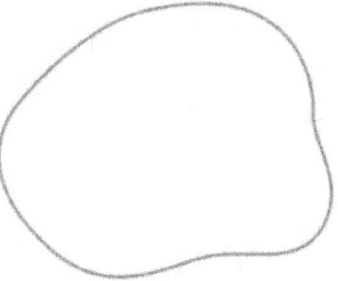

1) Draw a round shape for the head closer to the right edge of the sheet.

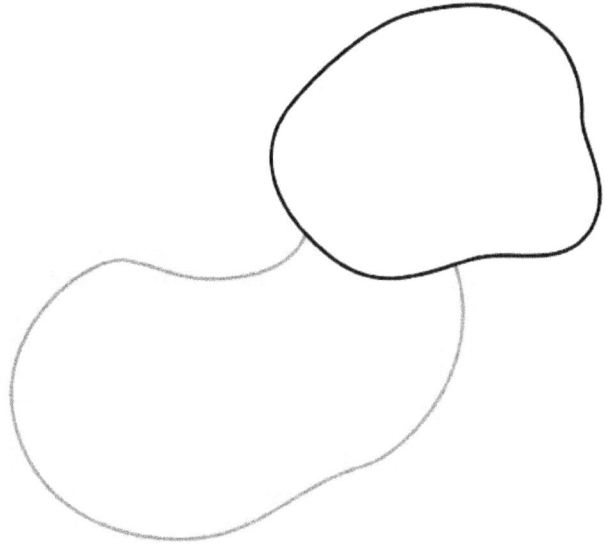

2) Draw an extended body right under the head, as shown in the example.

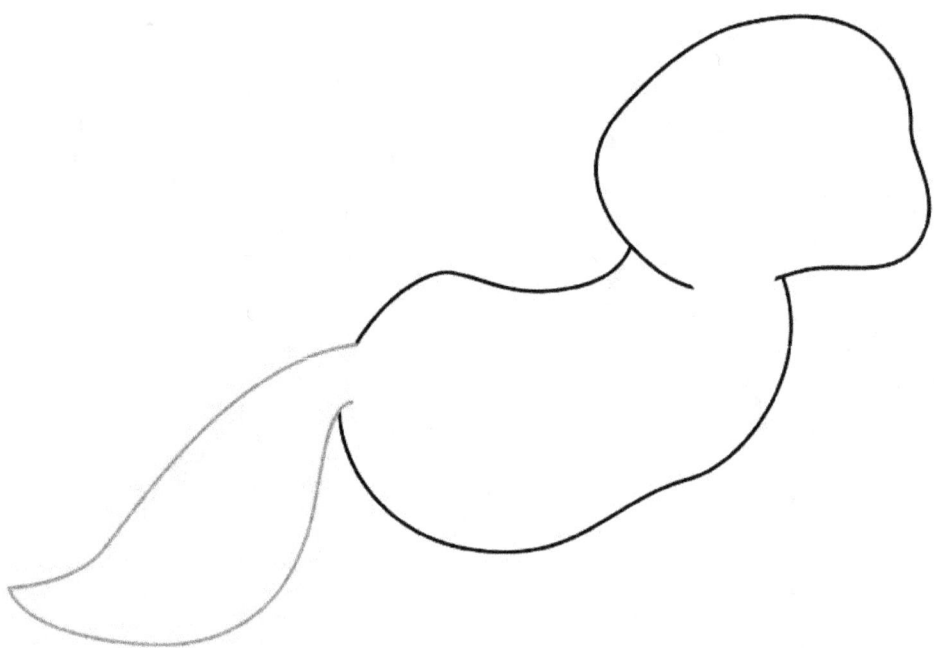

3) Draw a long tail on the left side.

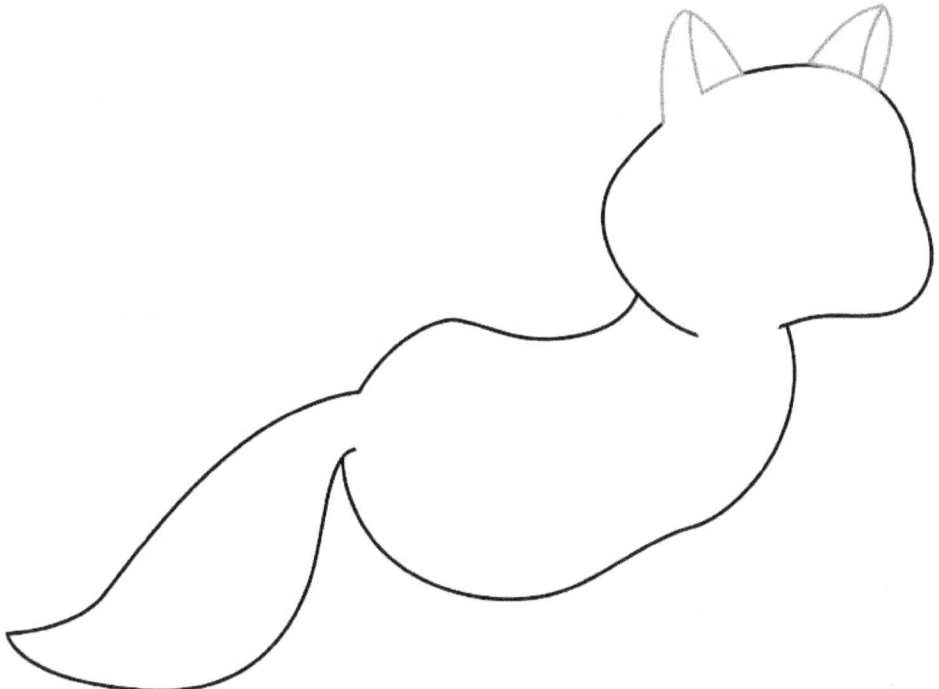

4) Draw two ears on the head.

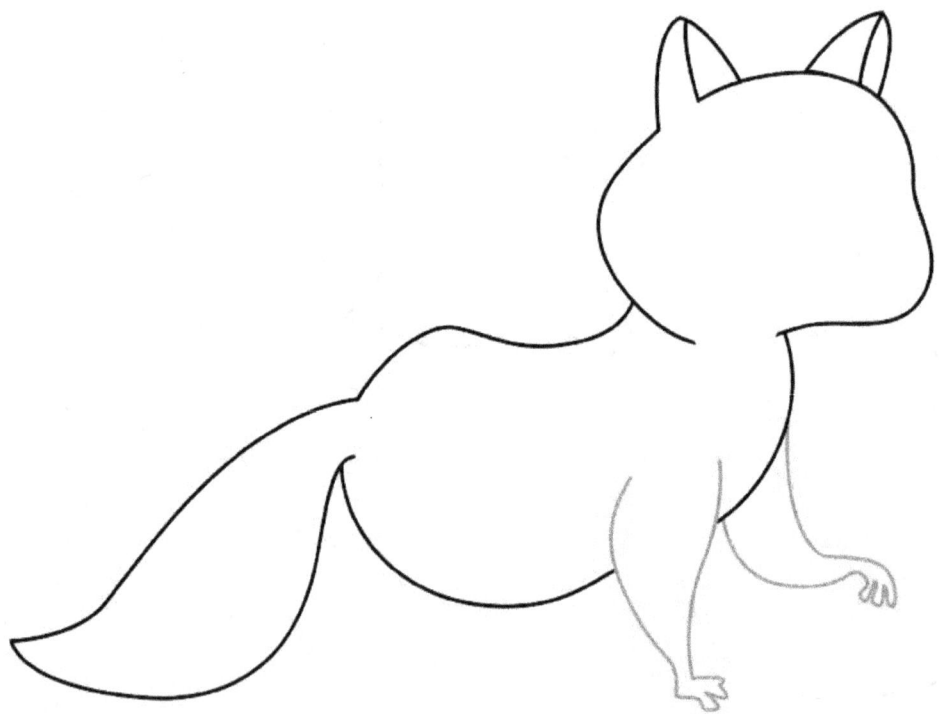

5) Draw the front paws.

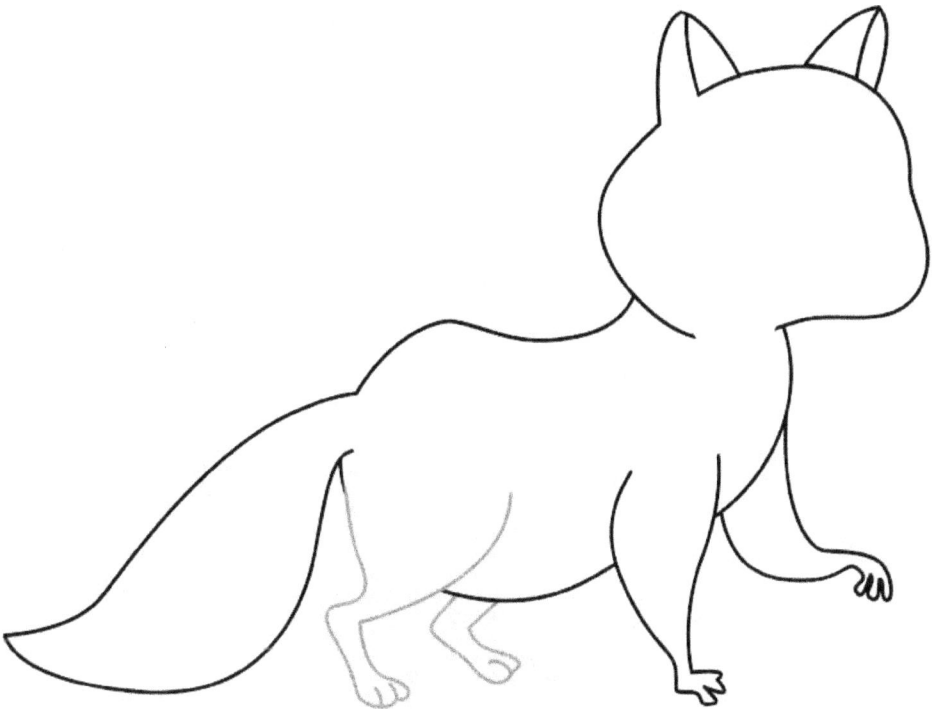

6) Draw hind legs, be close to the original.

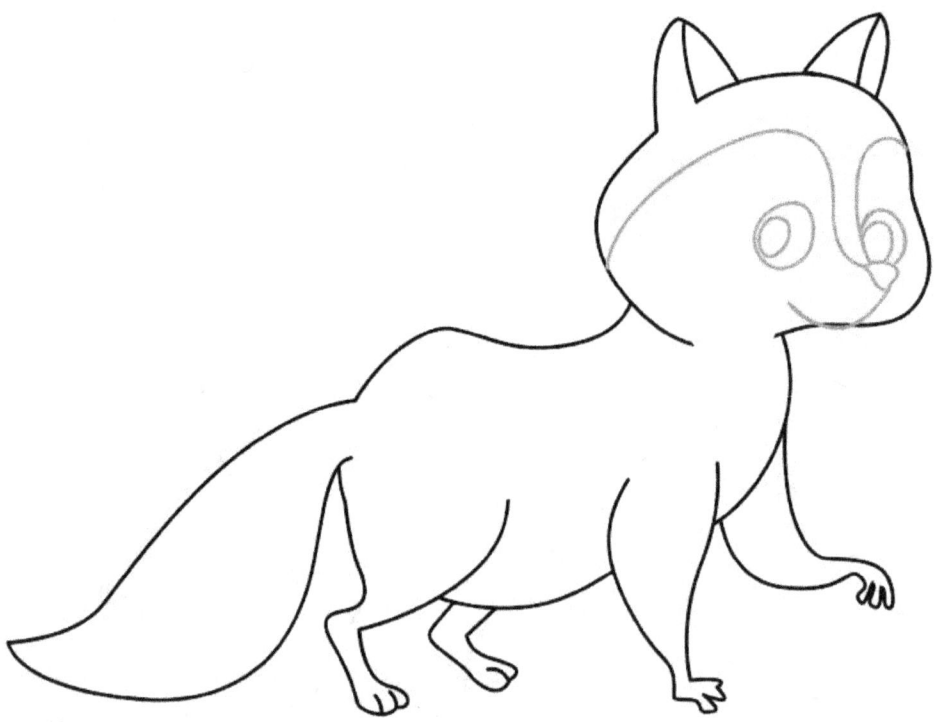

7) Draw the face of a raccoon - eyes, nose and mouth.

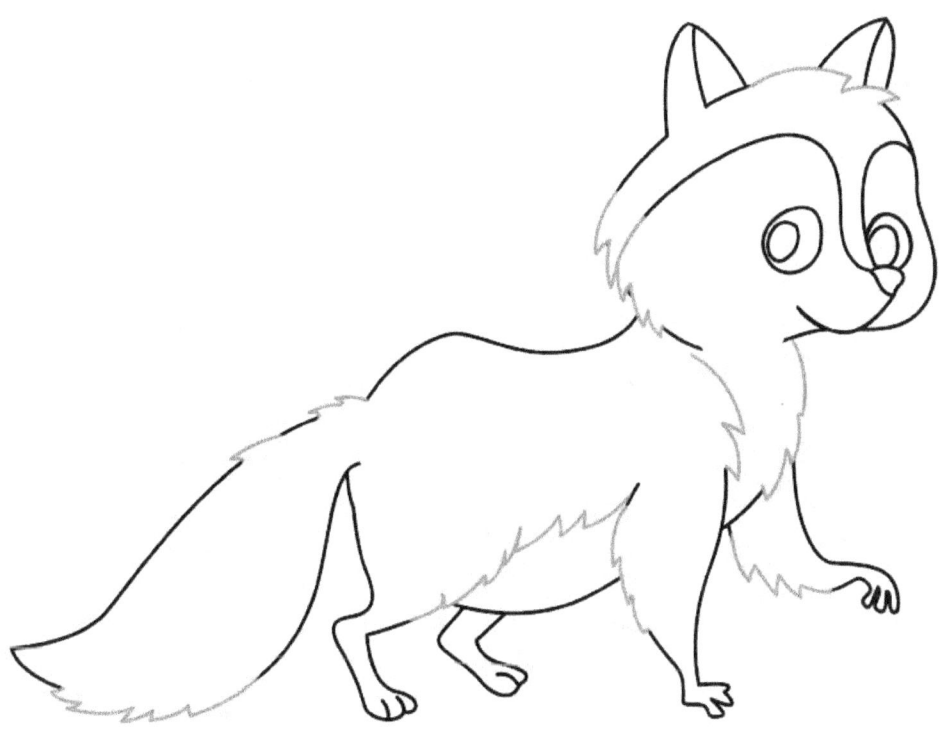

8) Add fluffy fur in several places.

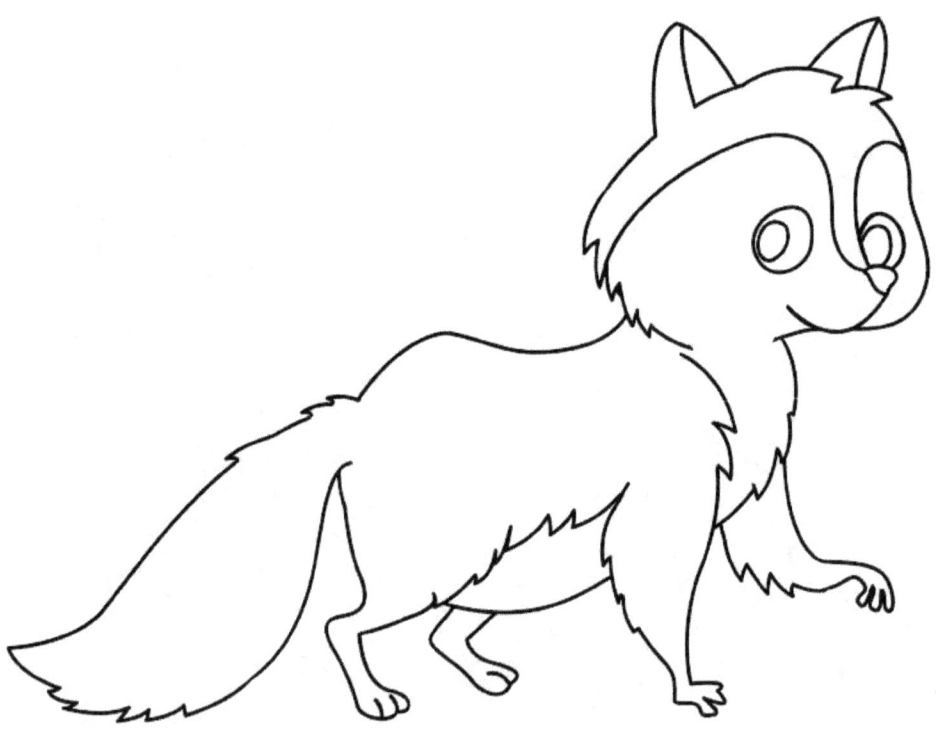

9) Done, let's start coloring!

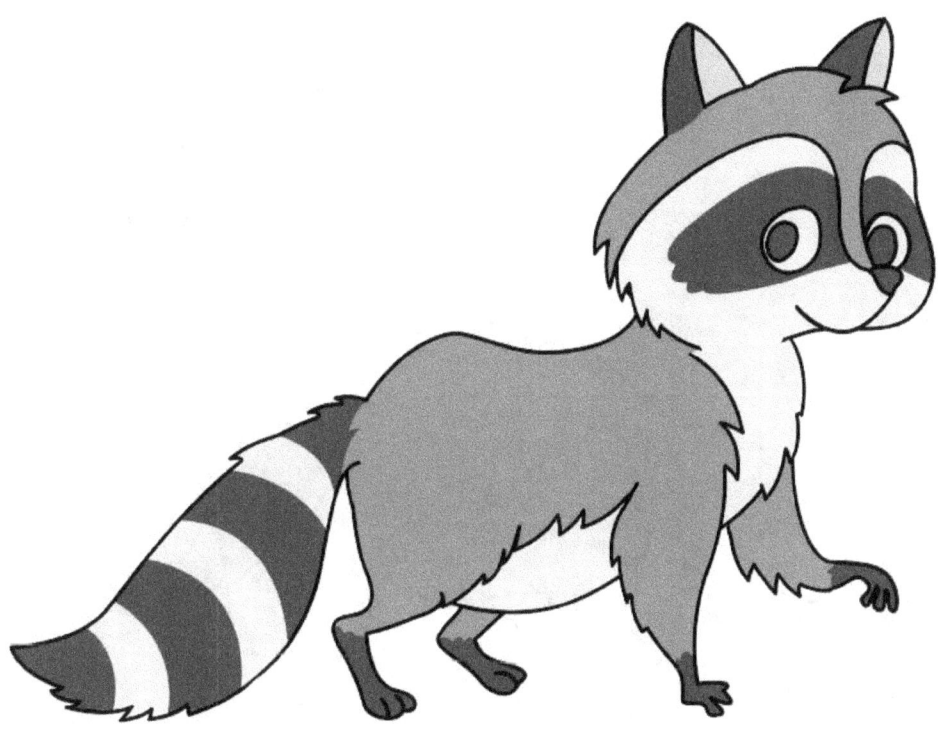

10) Color picture using grey, black and white for fur.

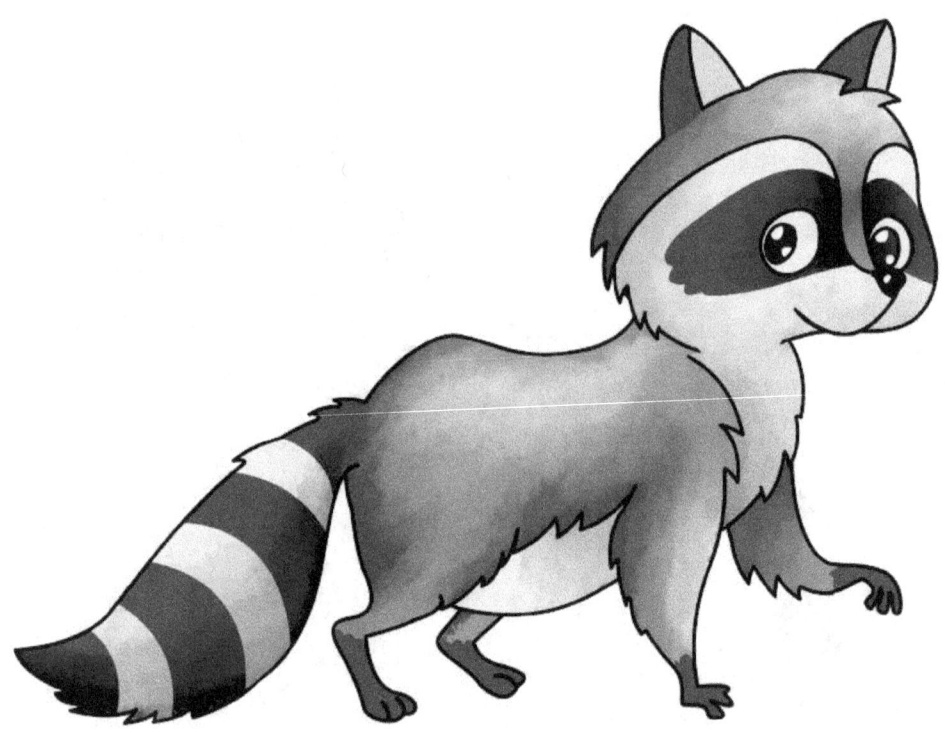

11) Add some shadows and highlights to add volume.

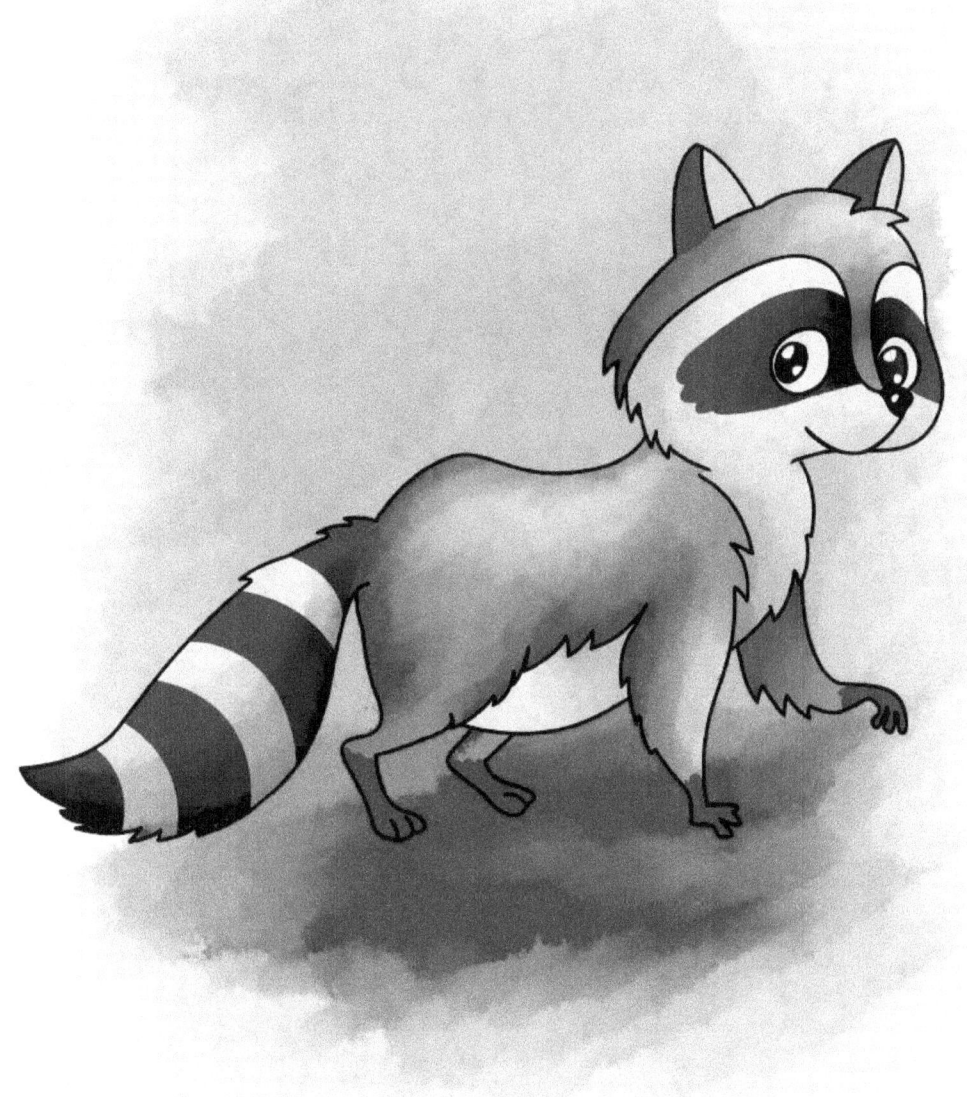

12) Colored version.

How to draw Racoon3

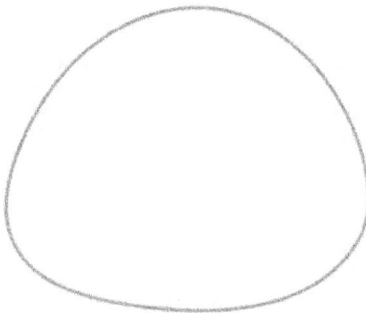

1) Draw a round head in the center of the sheet.

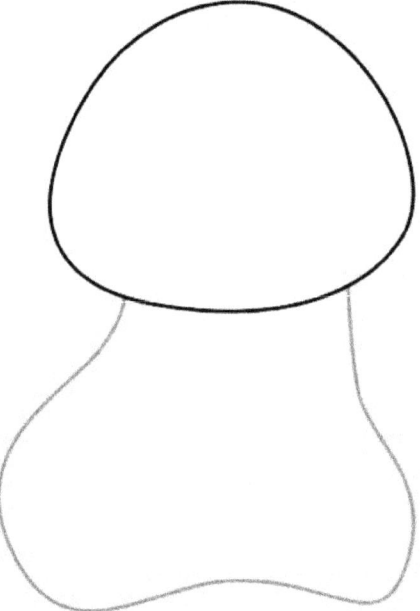

2) Add the body below, as shown in the example.

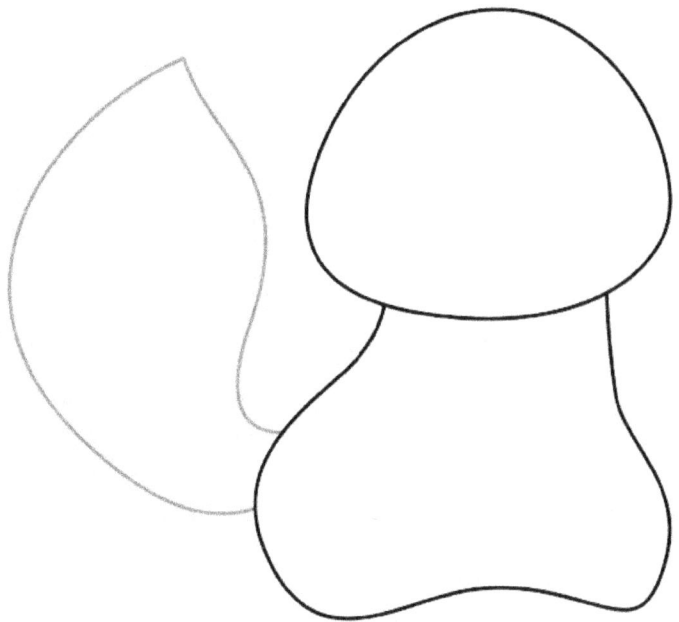

3) Draw a big fluffy tail on the left side.

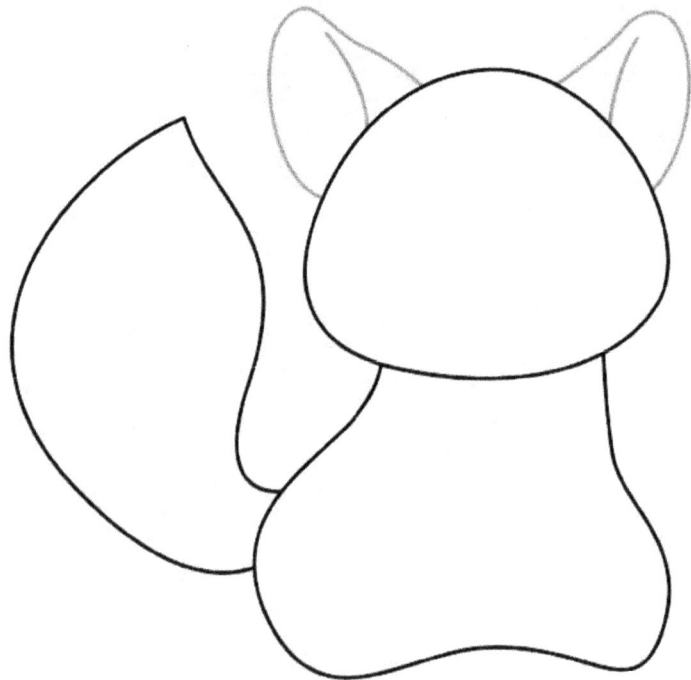

4) Draw two ears on the head.

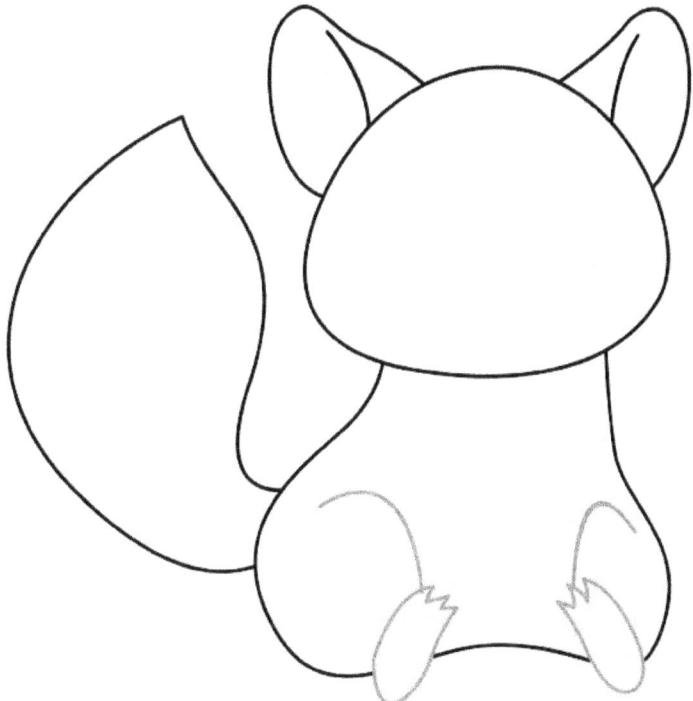

5) Draw the hind legs in a sitting posture.

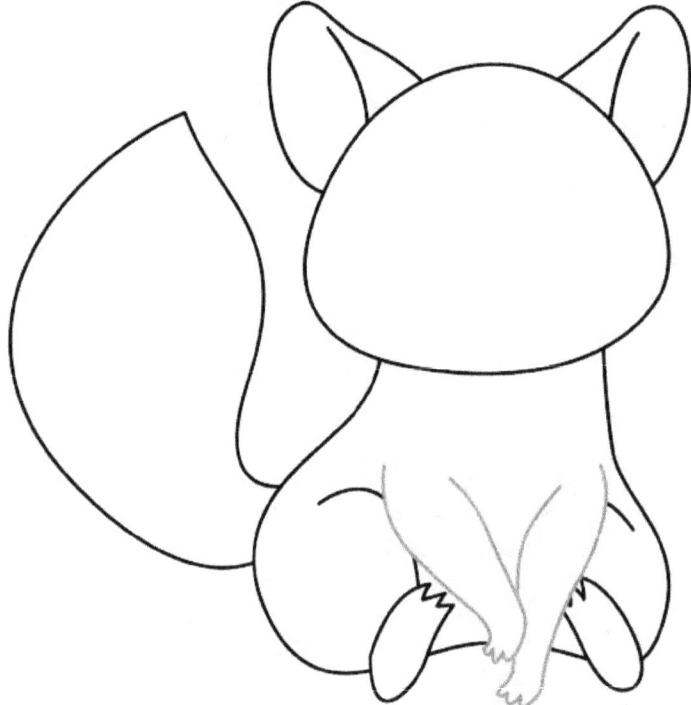

6) Draw the front paws, be close to the original.

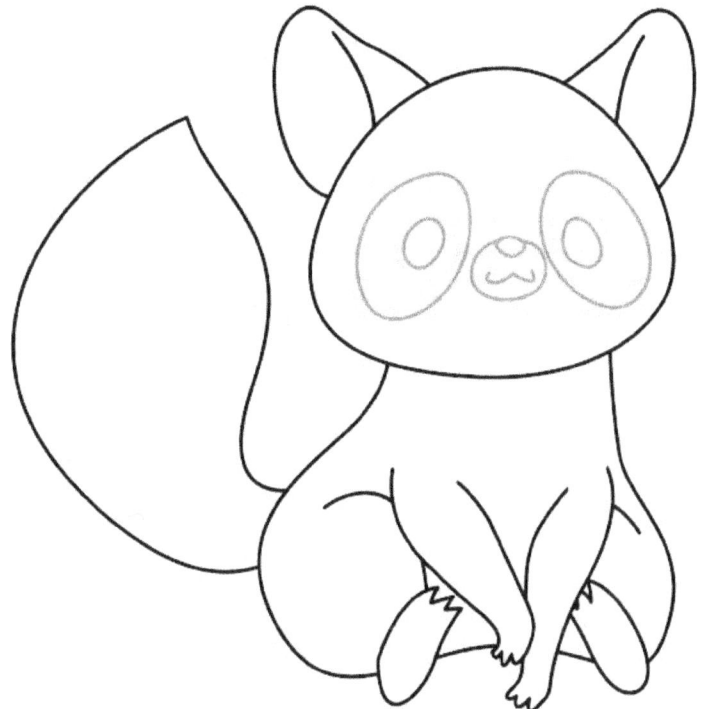

7) Draw the nose, mouth, eyes and large circles around them.

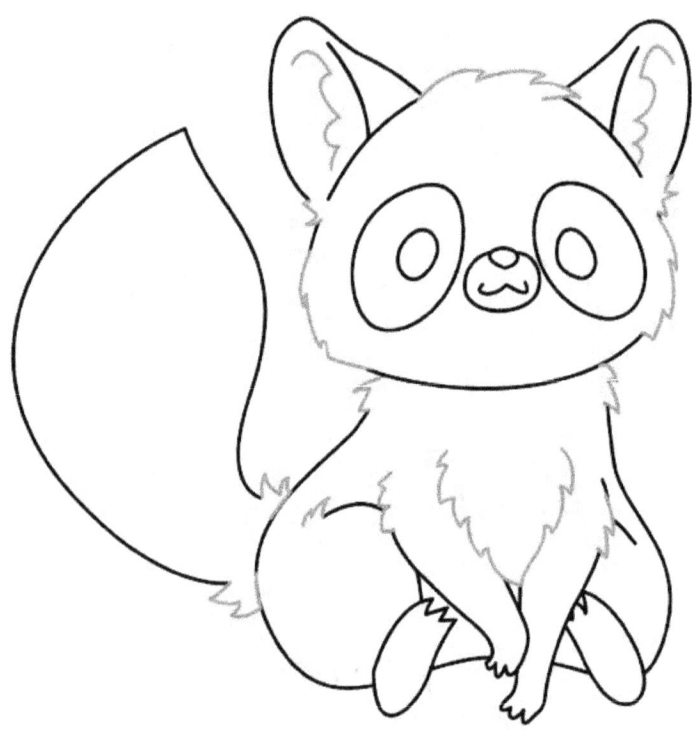

8) Add fluffy fur to the body.

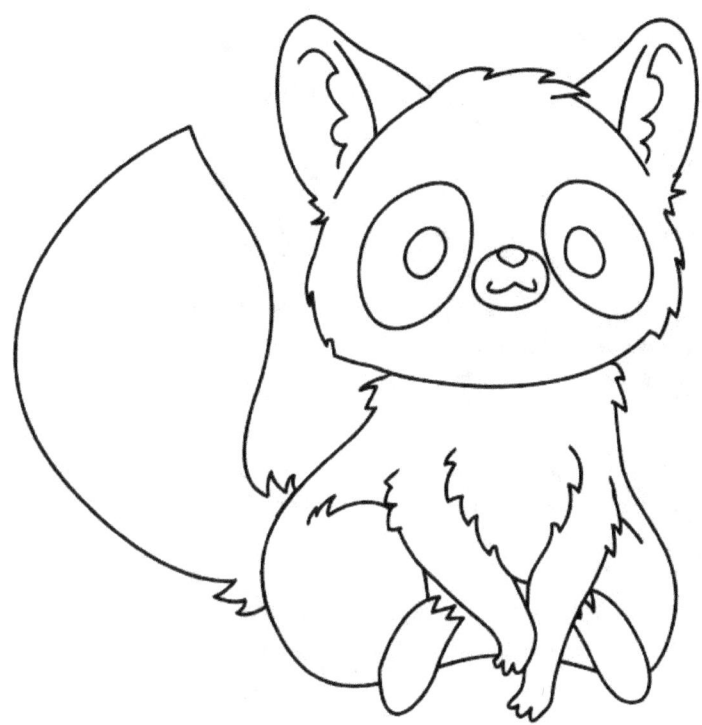

9) Done, let's start coloring!

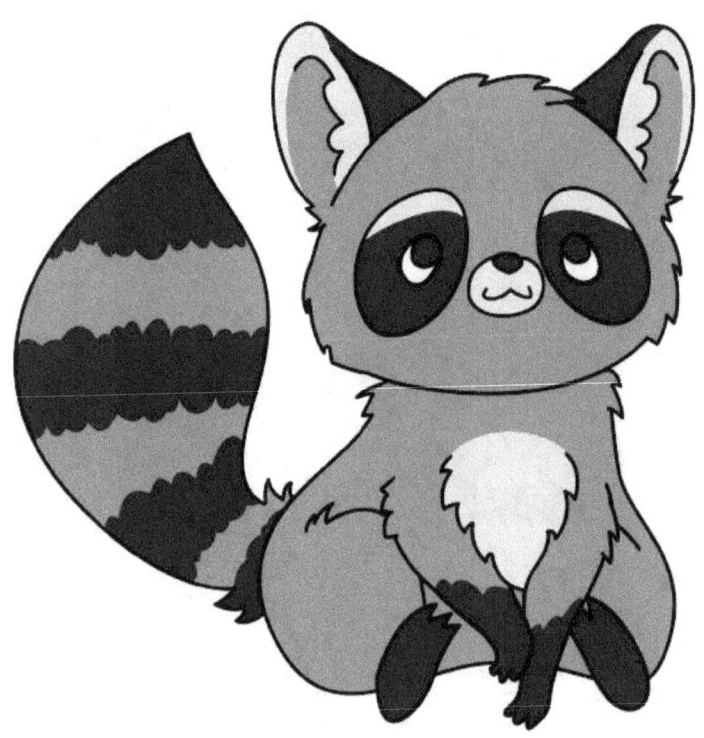

10) Color picture using grey, black and white for fur.

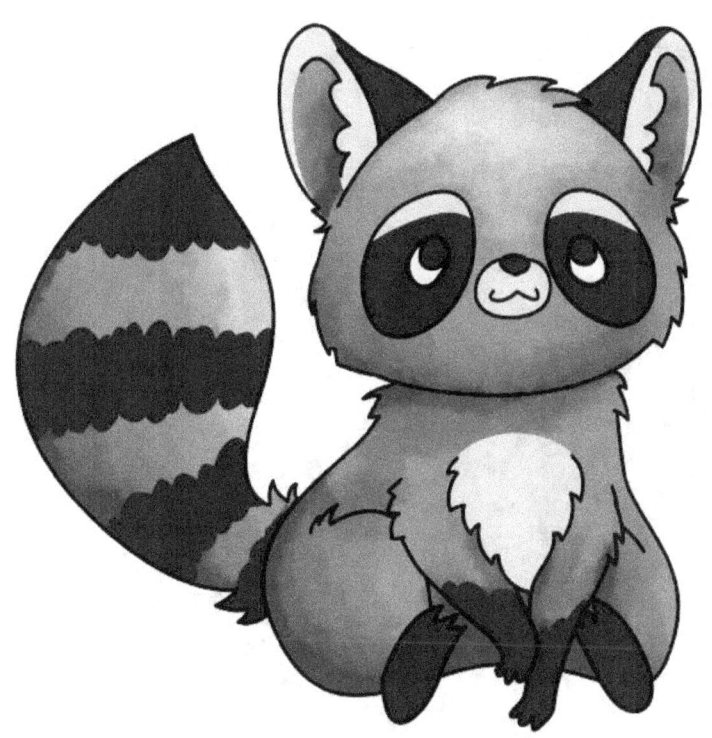

11) Add some shadows and highlights to add volume.

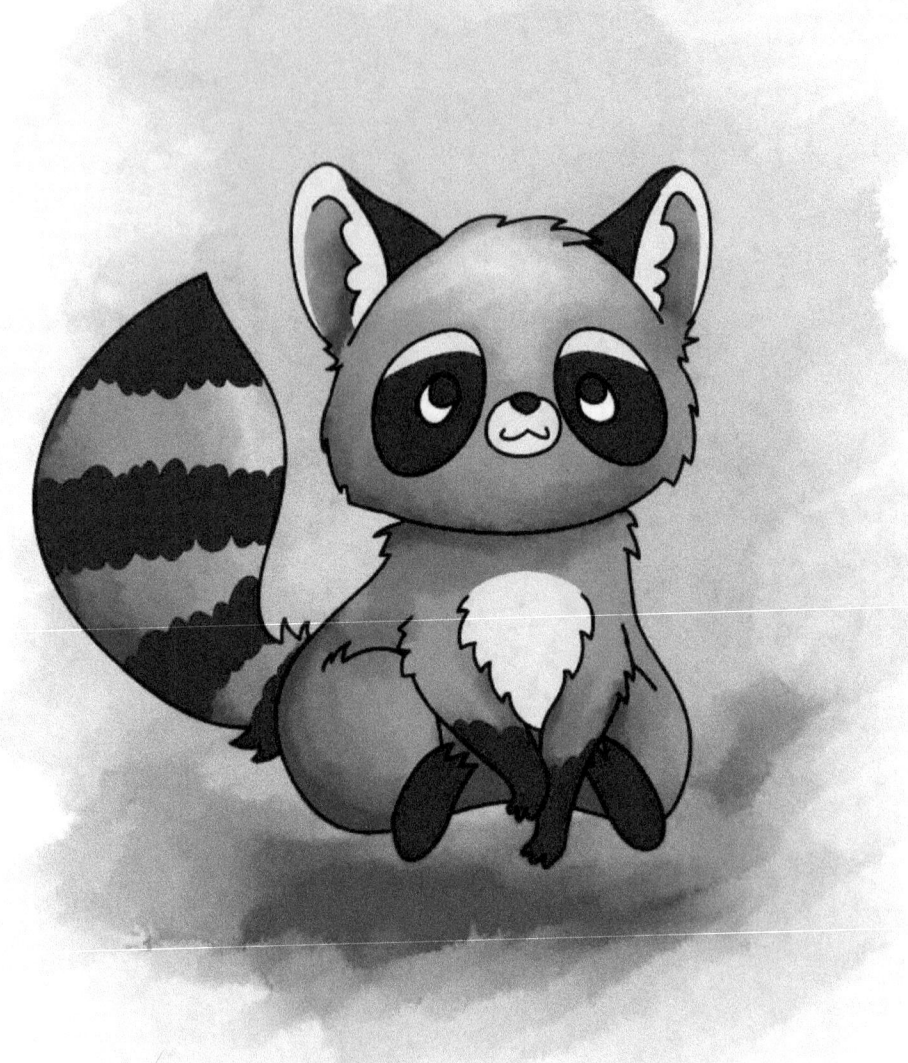

12) Colored version.

How to draw Racoon4

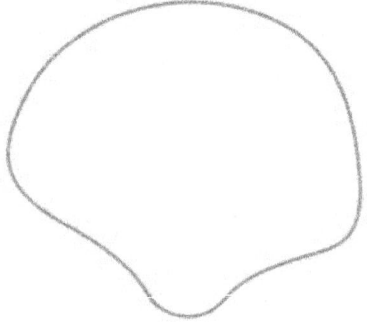

1) Draw the head closer to the right edge of the sheet.

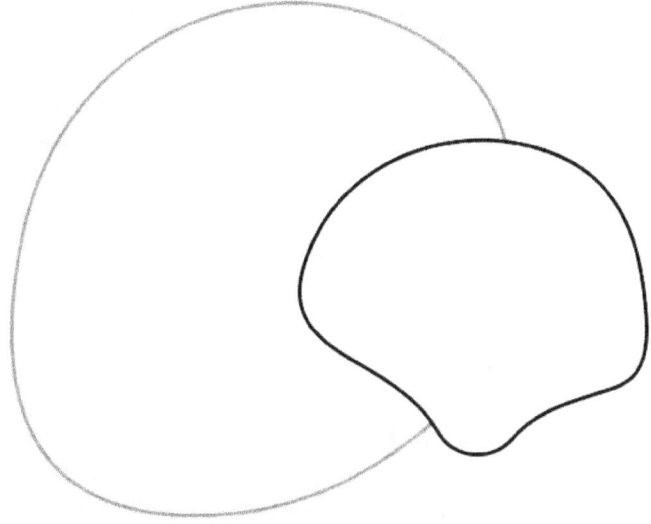

2) Add a large round body shape in the center of the sheet behind the head.

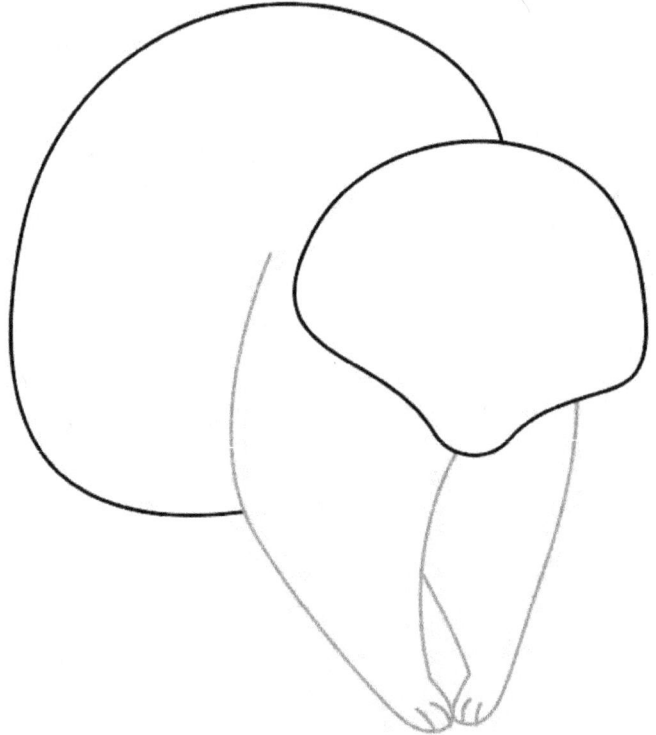

3) Draw the front paws under the head.

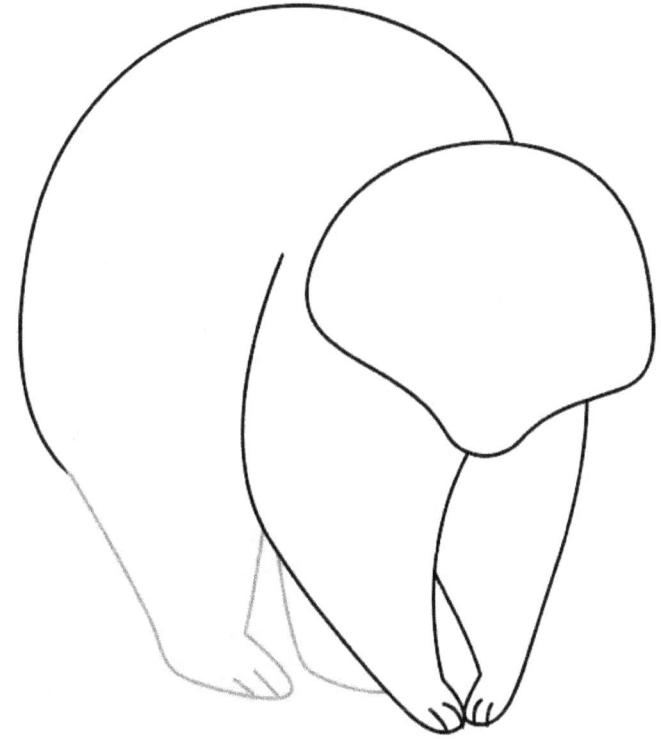

4) Draw hind legs under the body.

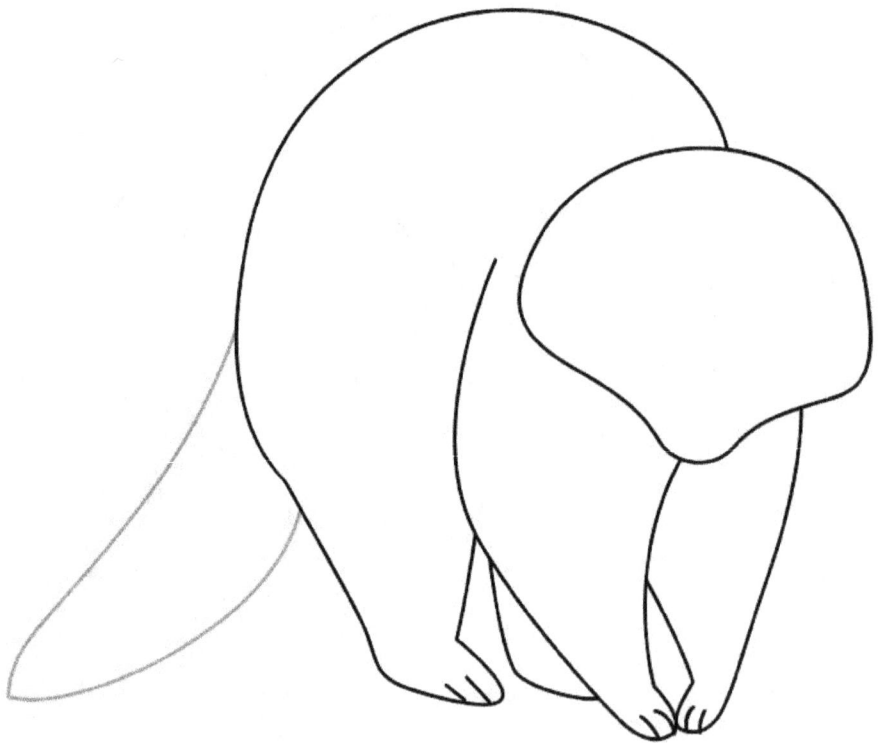

5) Draw the tail on the left side.

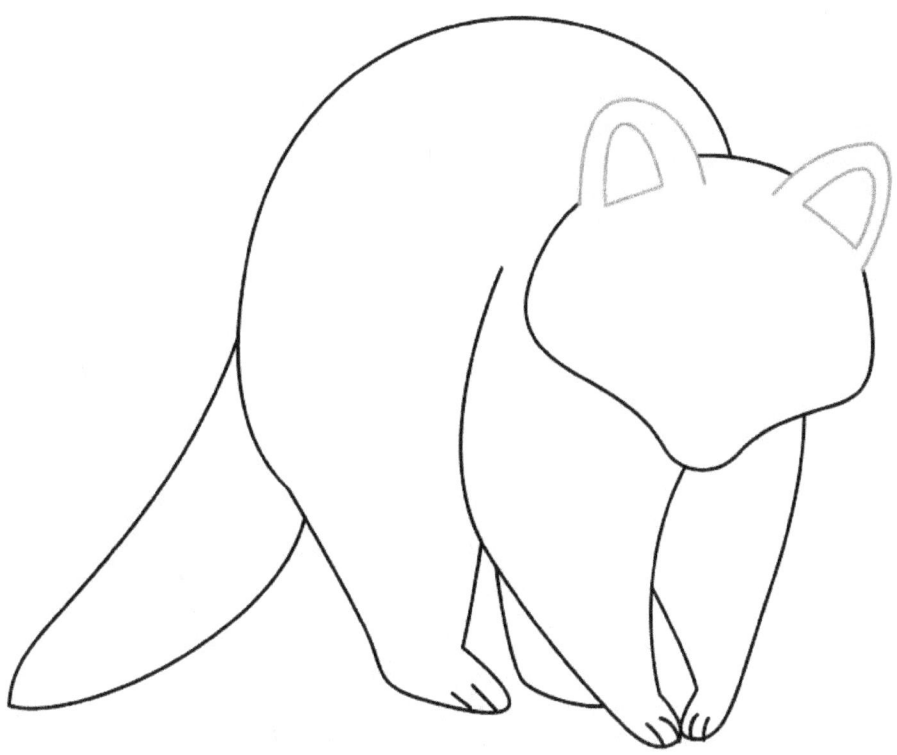

6) Draw two ears on the head.

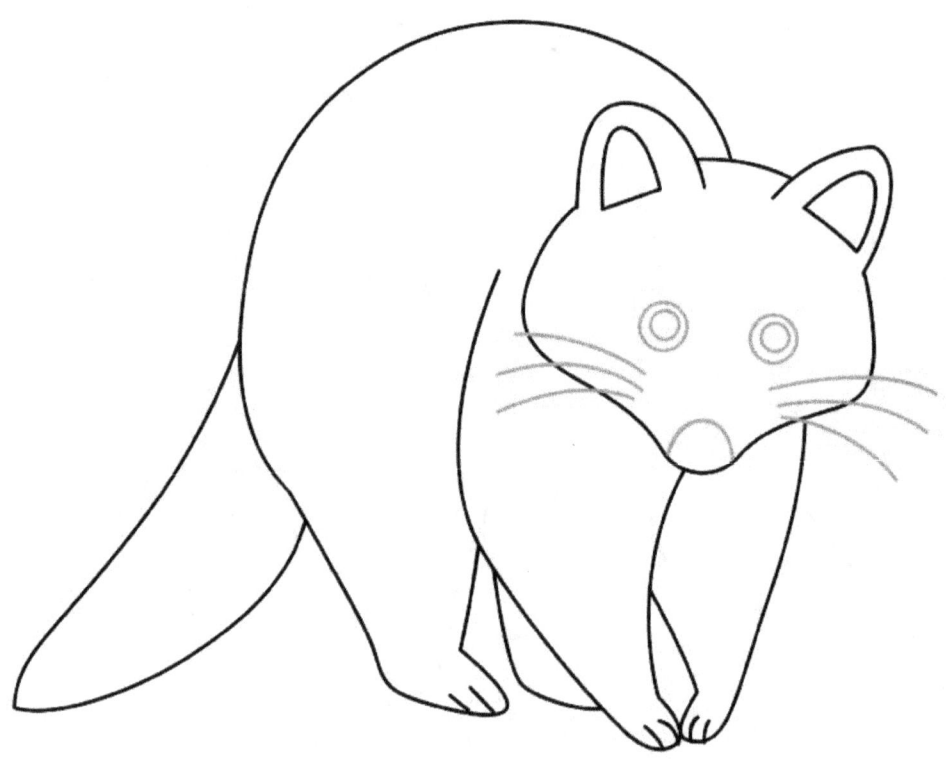

7) Add eyes, nose and antennae to face.

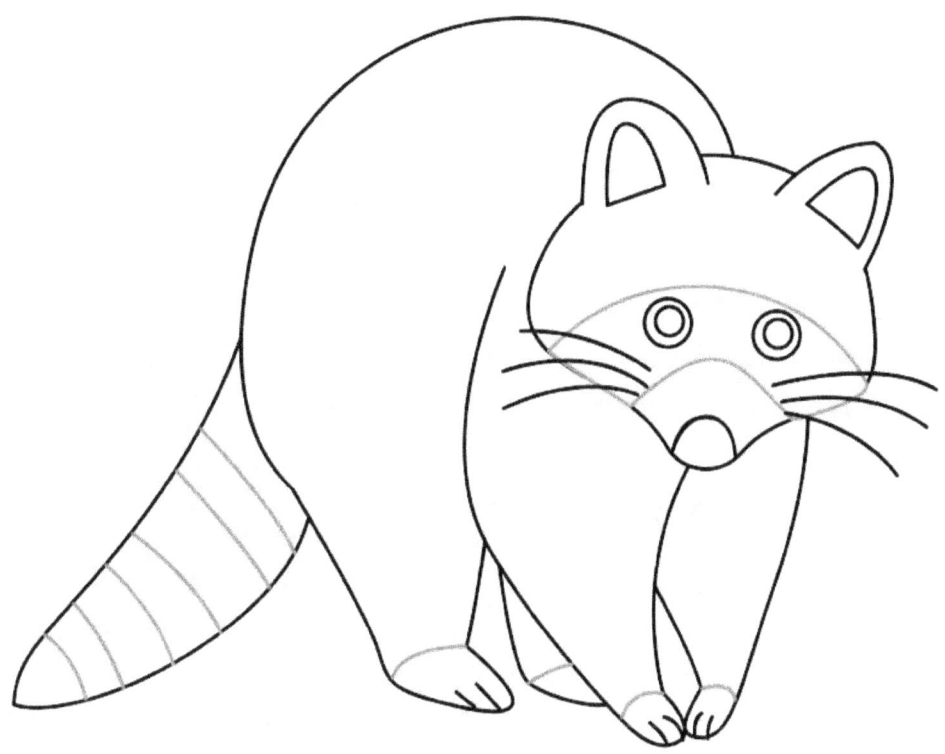

8) Add on the body a few bands in the tail, legs and face.

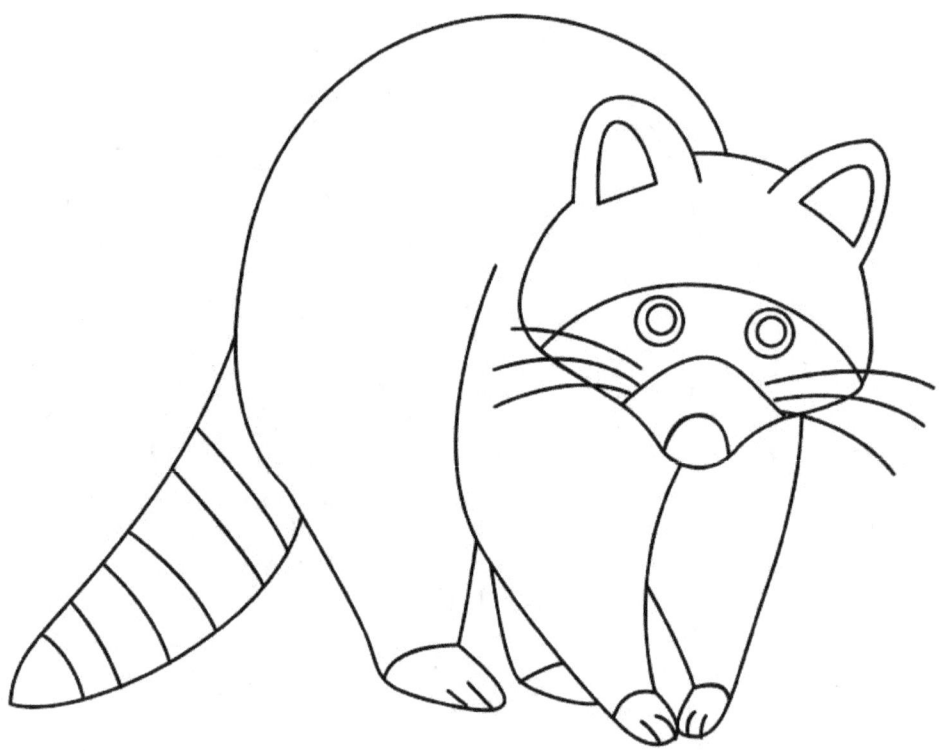

9) Done, let's start coloring!

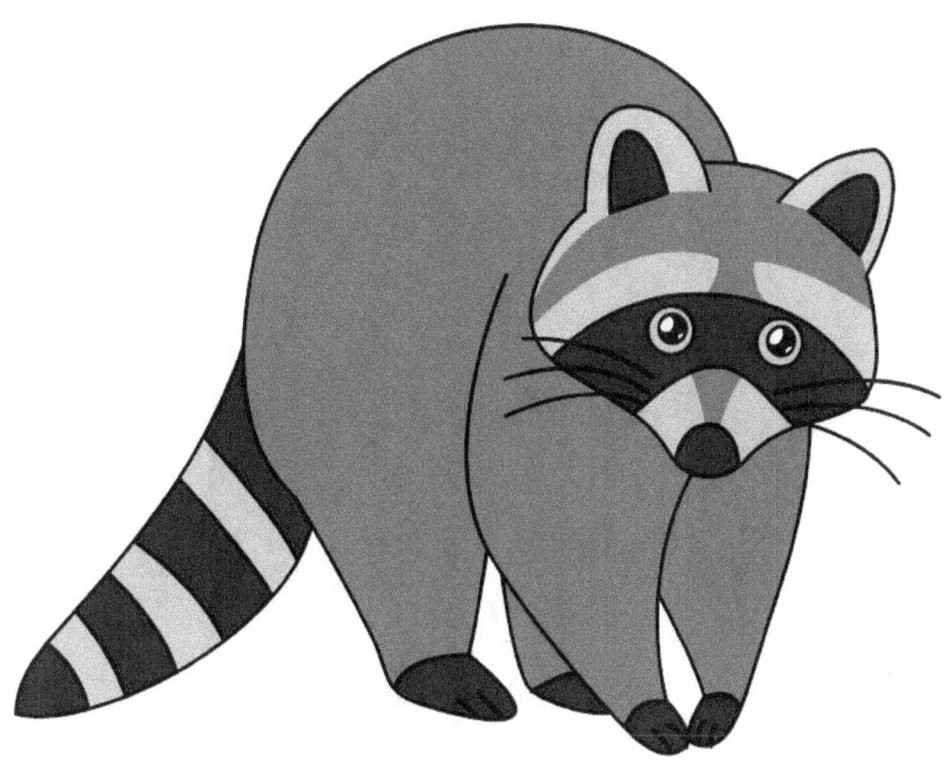

10) Color picture using grey, black and white for fur.

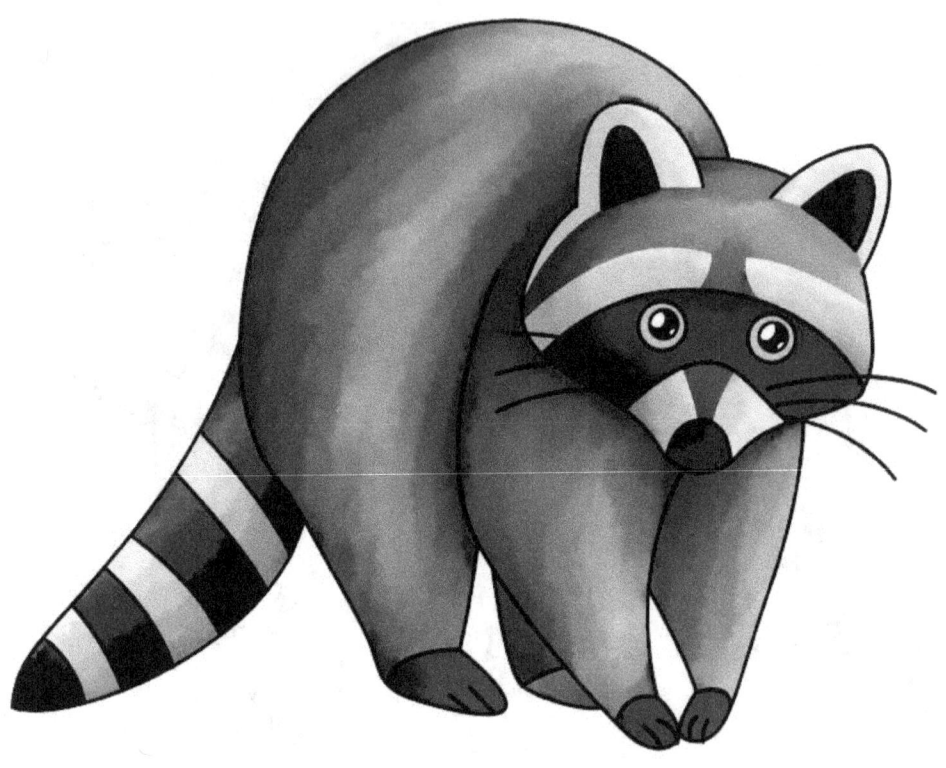

11) Add some shadows and highlights to add volume.

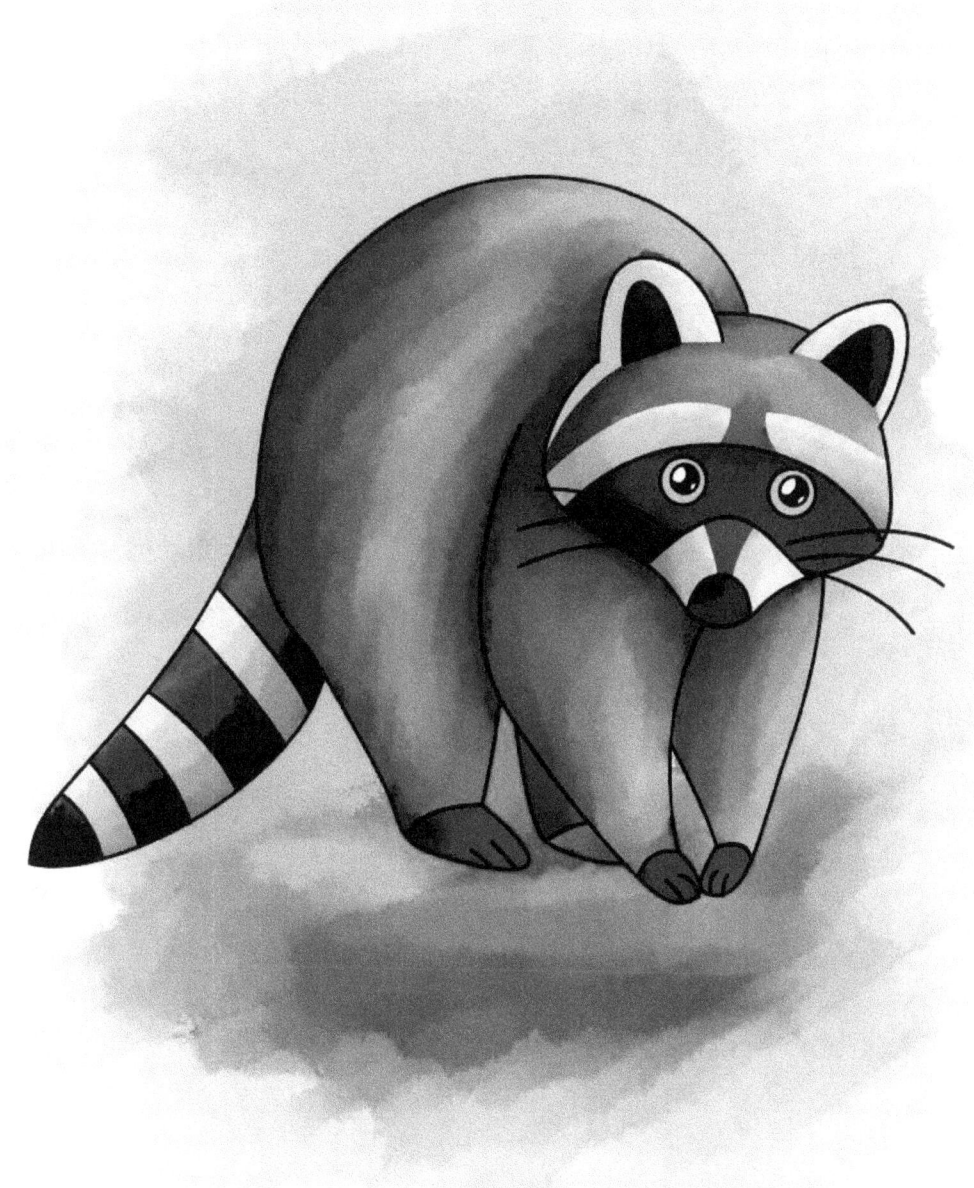

12) Colored version.

How to draw Racoon5

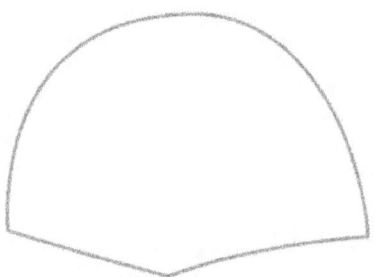

1) Draw the head closer to the left edge of the sheet.

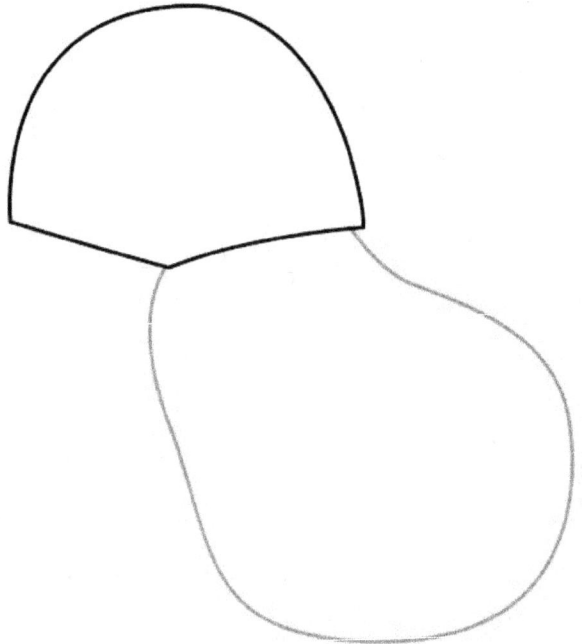

2) Add a body just below and to the right.

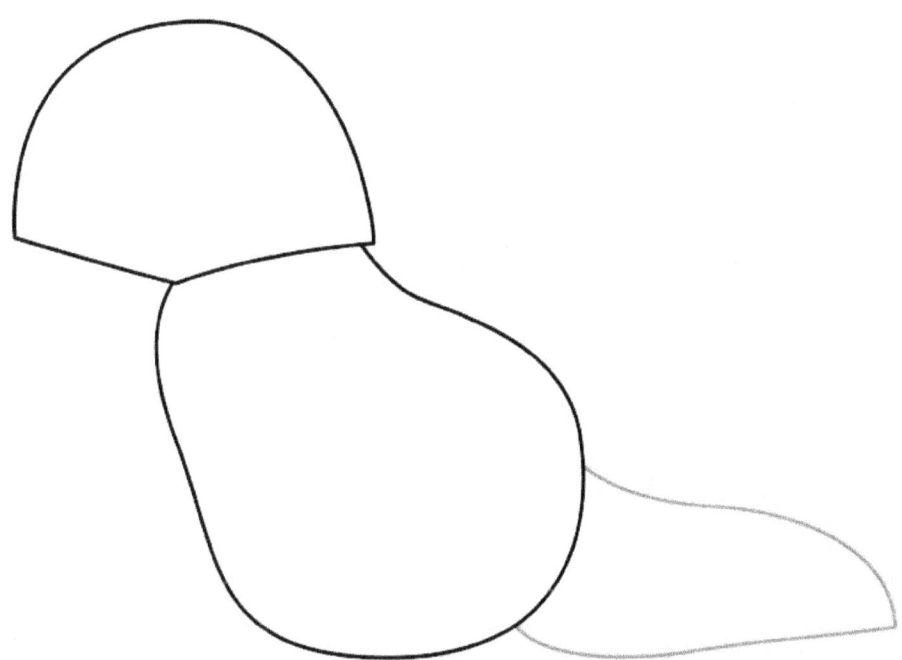

3) Draw a fluffy tail on the right.

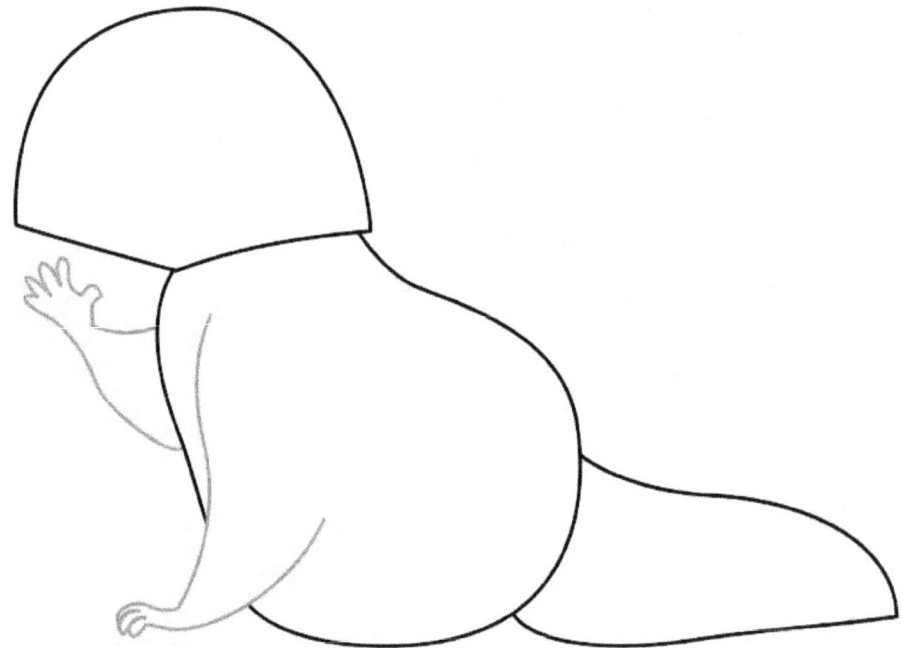

4) Draw the left front paws, as shown in the example.

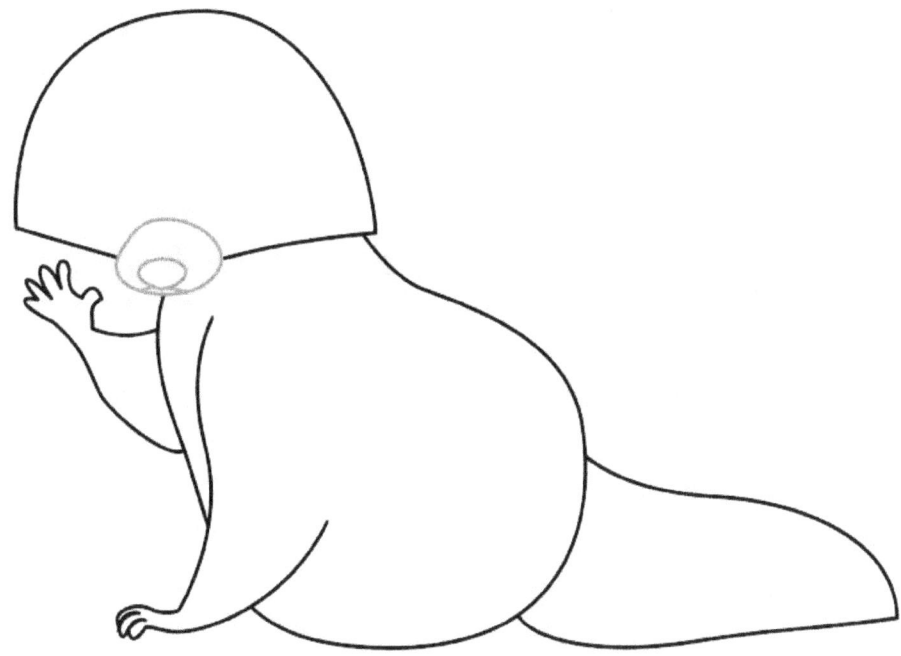

5) Add a stretched nose to the head, be close to the original.

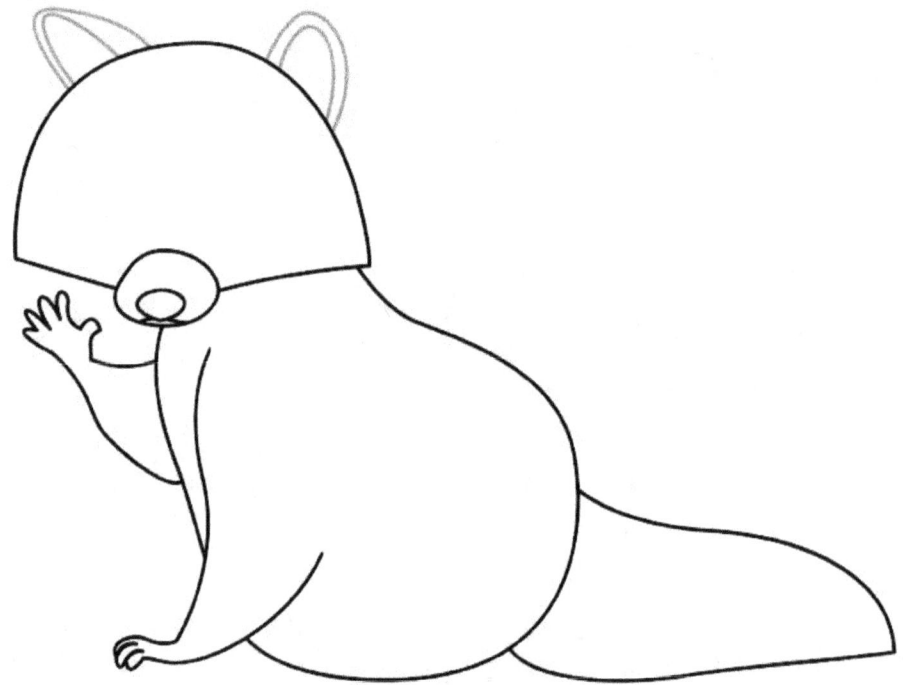

6) Draw two ears on the head.

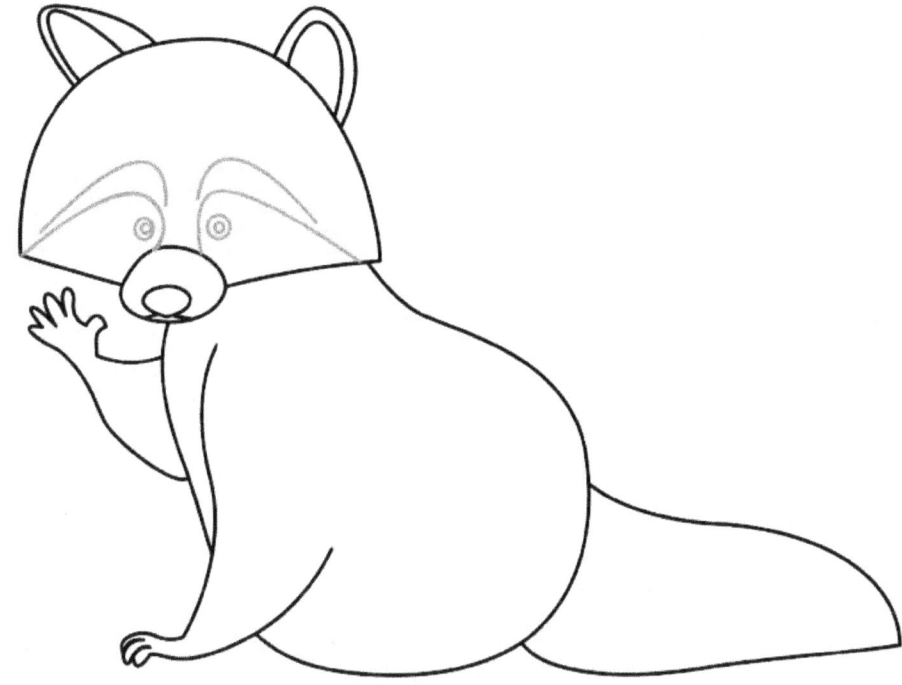

7) Add small eyes and streaks around the eyebrows on the head.

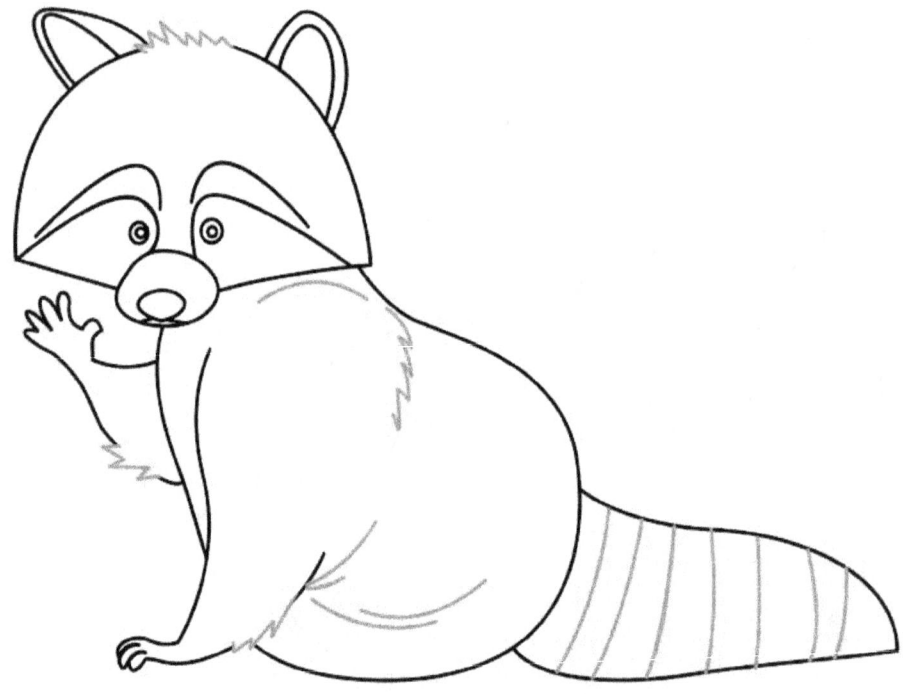

8) Draw stripes on the tail, add fluffy wool in several places.

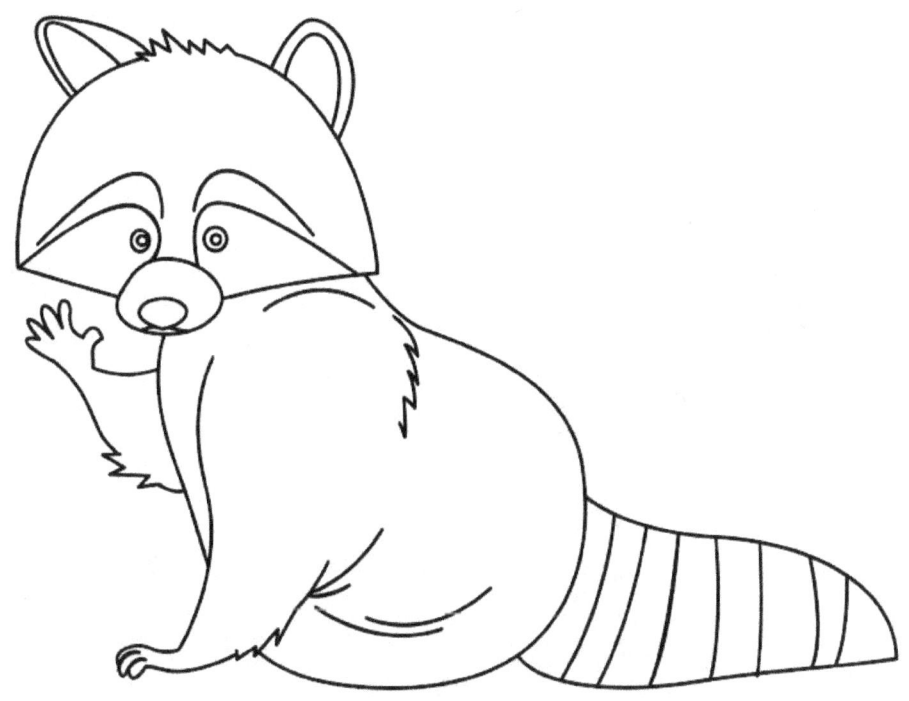

9) Done, let's start coloring!

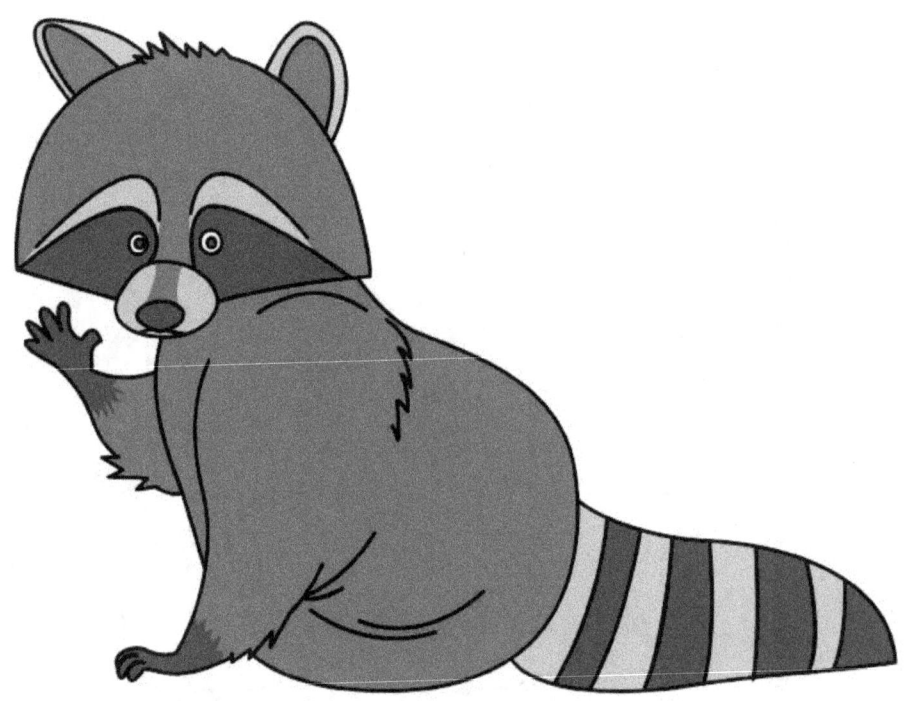

10) Color picture using grey and black for fur.

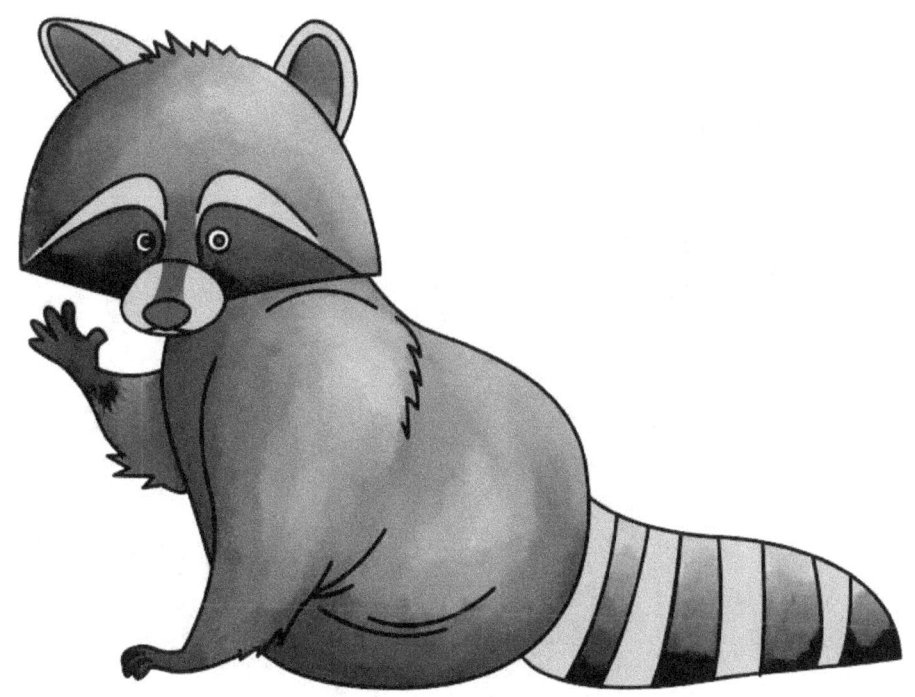

11) Add some shadows and highlights to add volume.

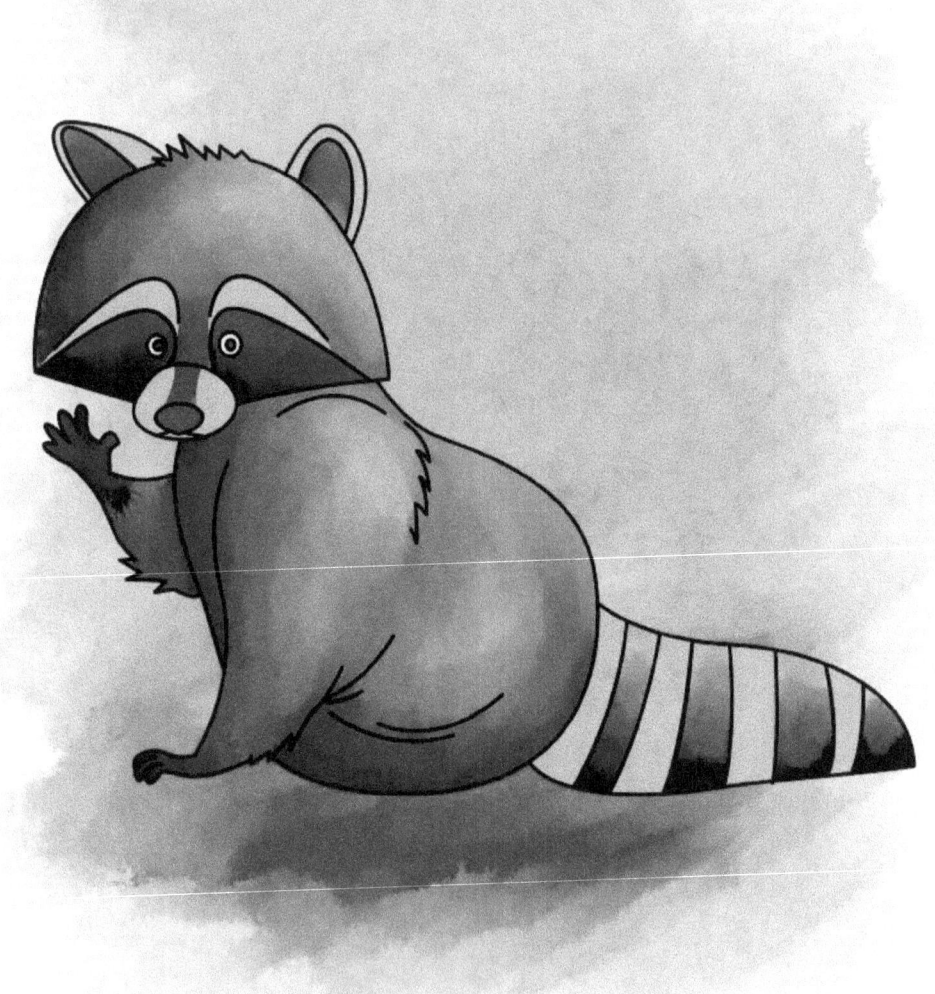

12) Colored version.

How to draw Racoon6

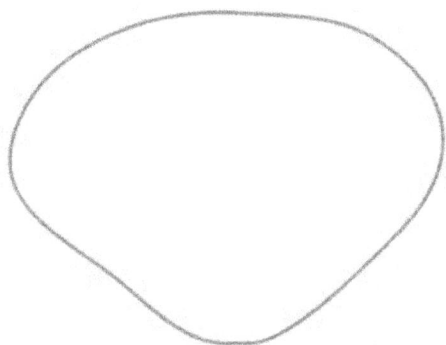

1) Draw the head in the center of the sheet.

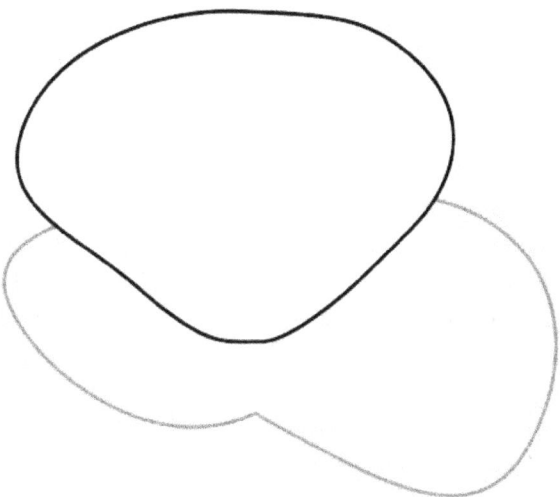

2) Add a figure for the body just below, be close to the original.

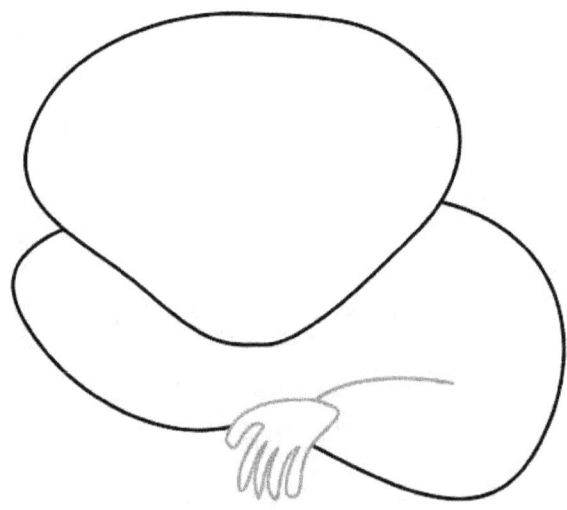

3) Draw a small palm, as shown in the example.

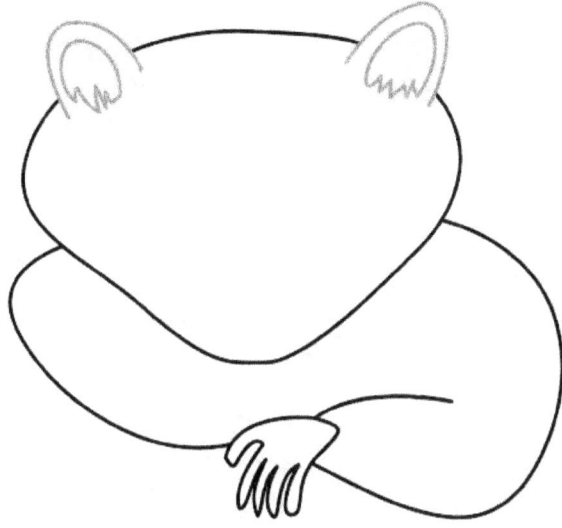

4) Draw two ears on the head.

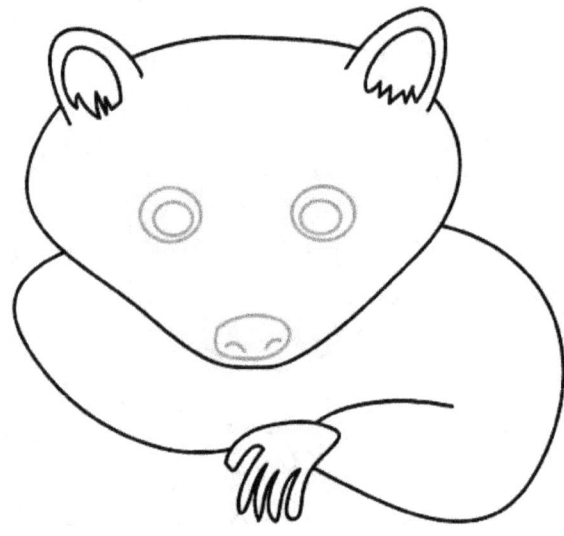

5) Draw two round eyes and a nose on the face.

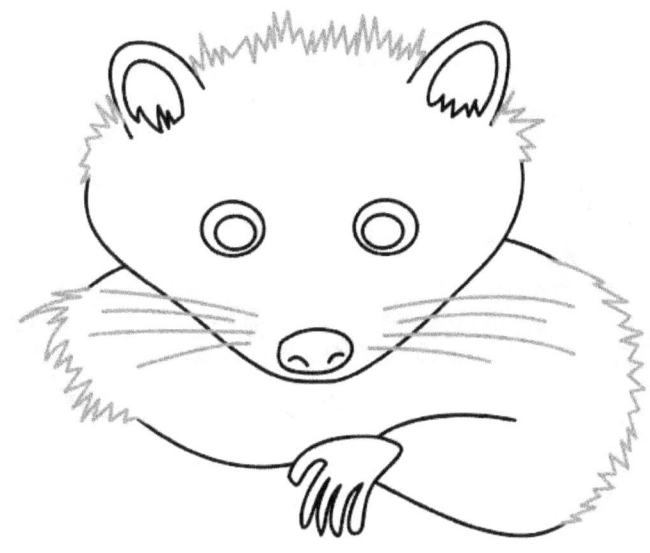

6) Add wool around the perimeter of the body.

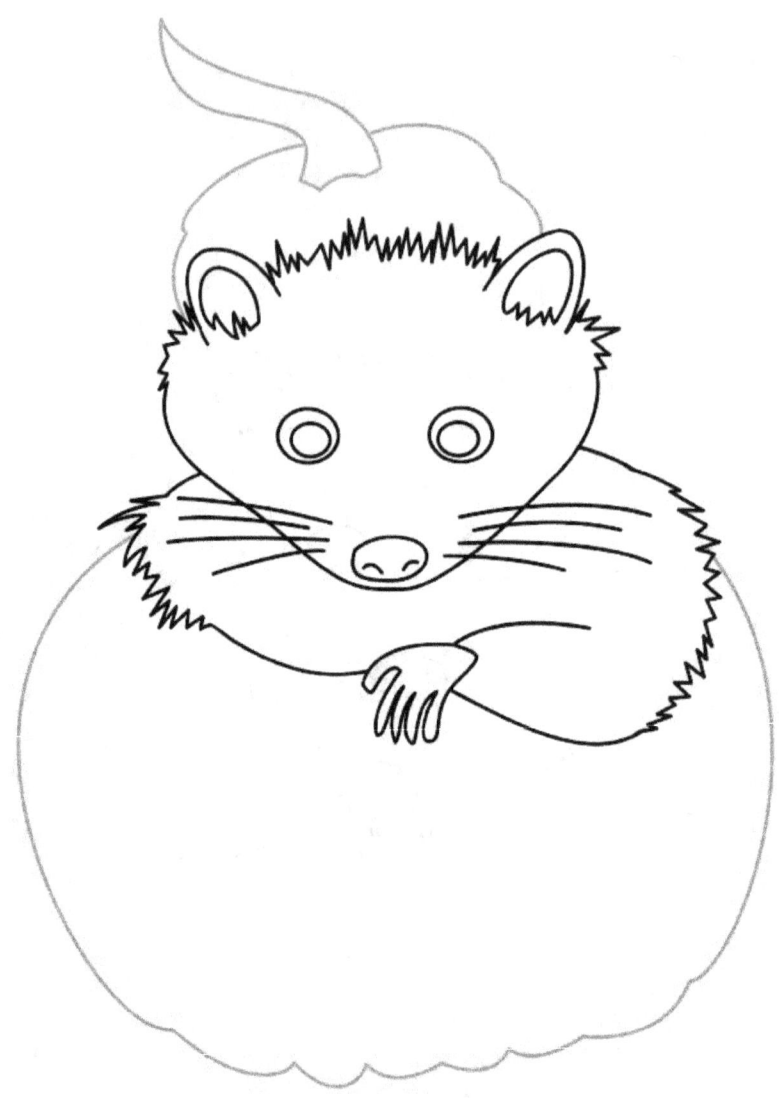

7) Draw a large circle for the pumpkin below the figure and the top of the pumpkin on the head.

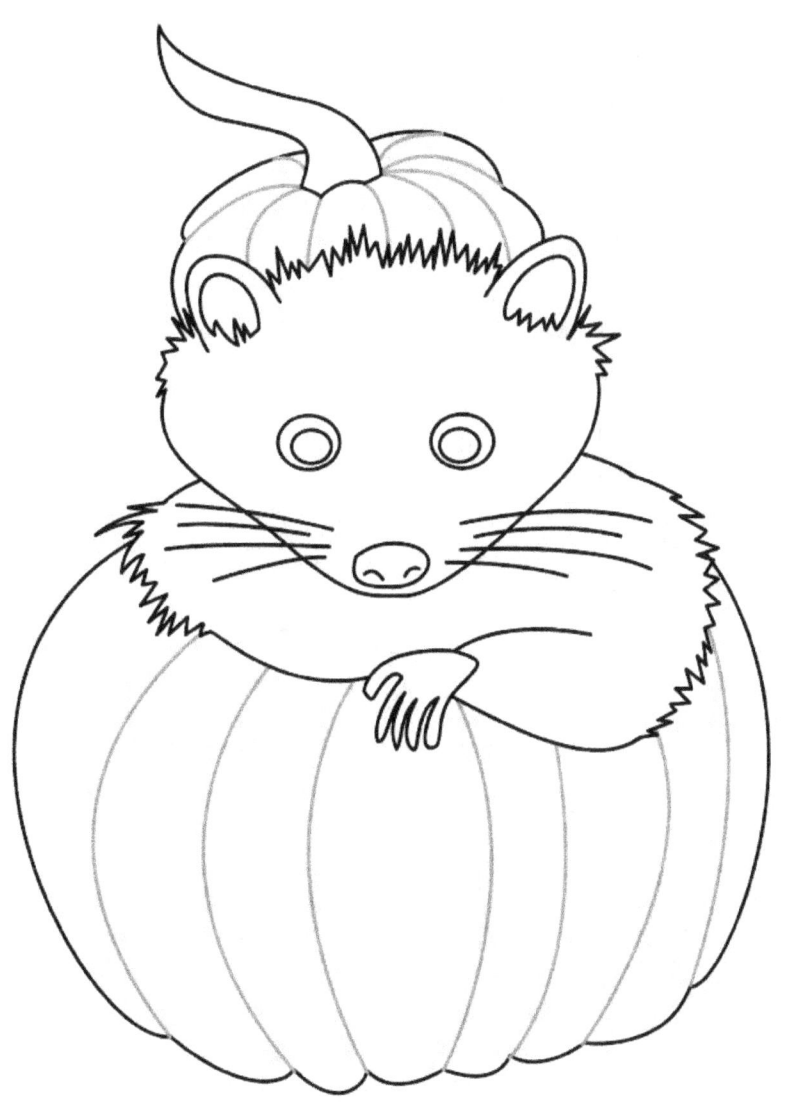

8) Add strips to the pumpkin.

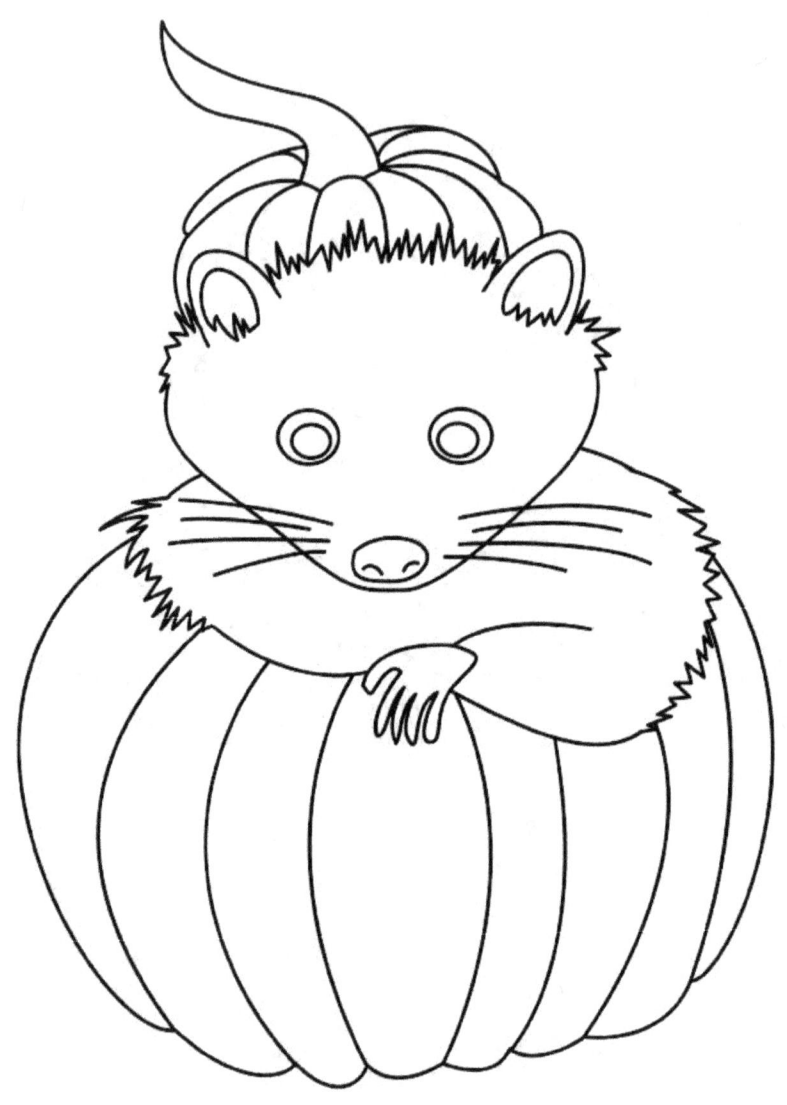

9) Done, let's start coloring!

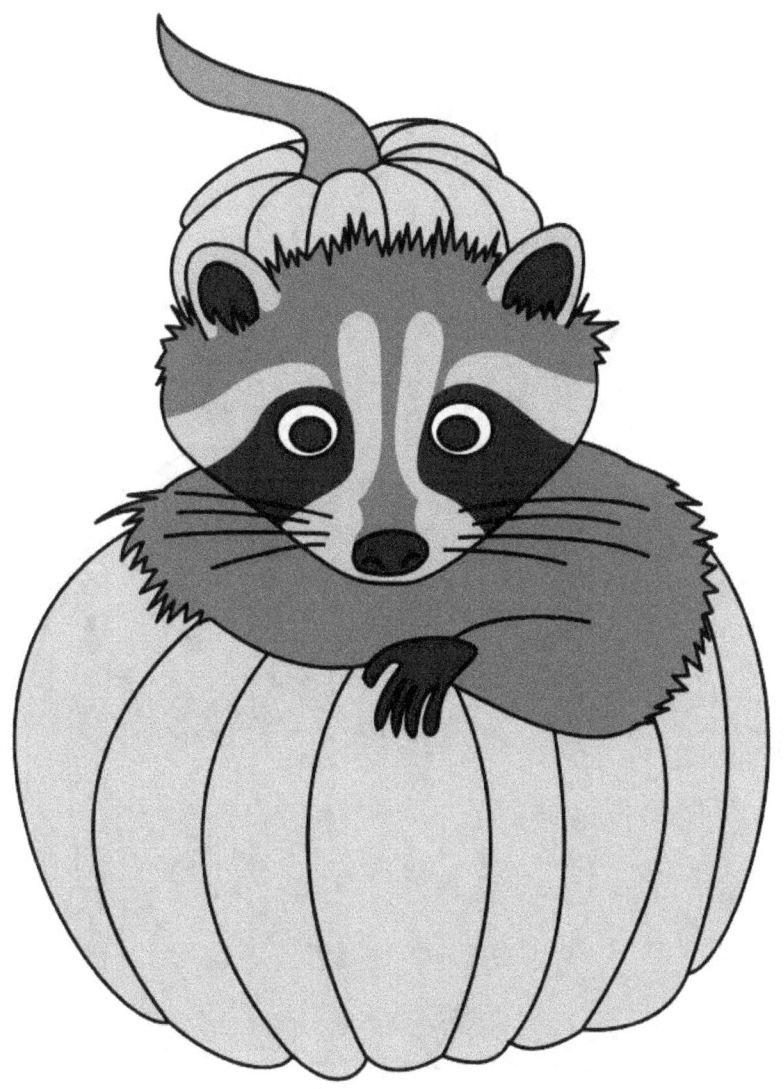

10) Color picture using grey and black for fur, orange for pumpkin.

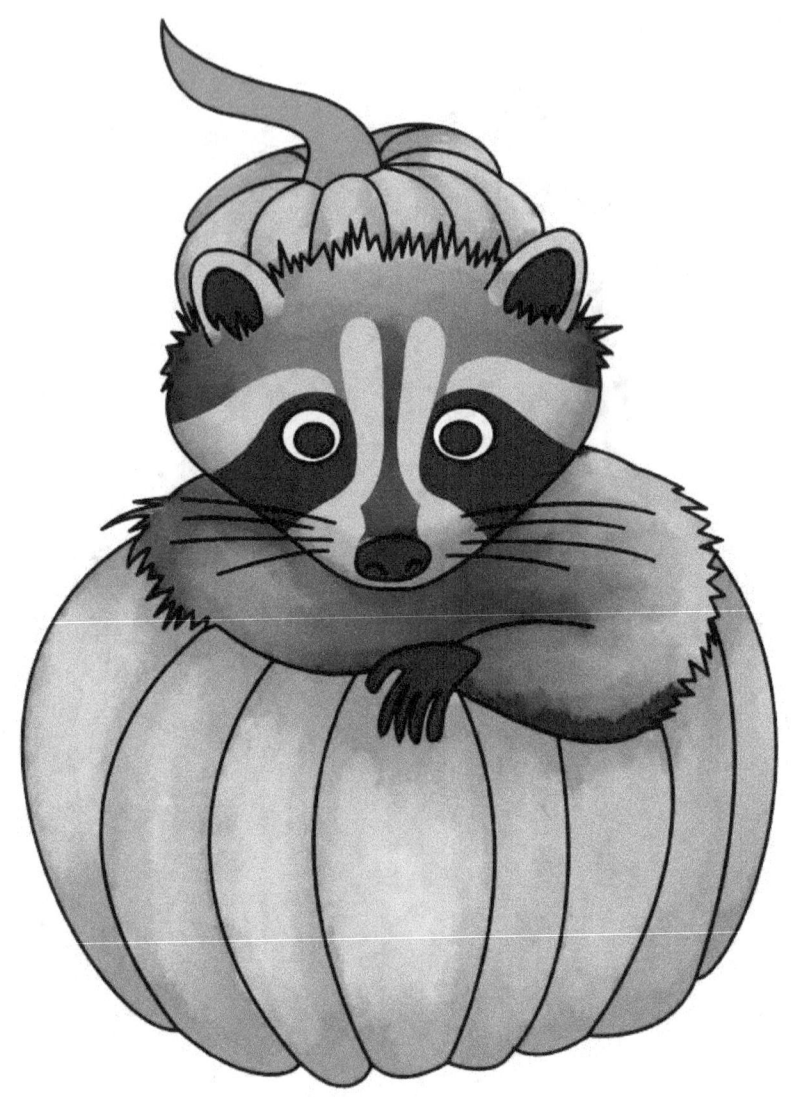

11) Add some shadows and highlights to add volume.

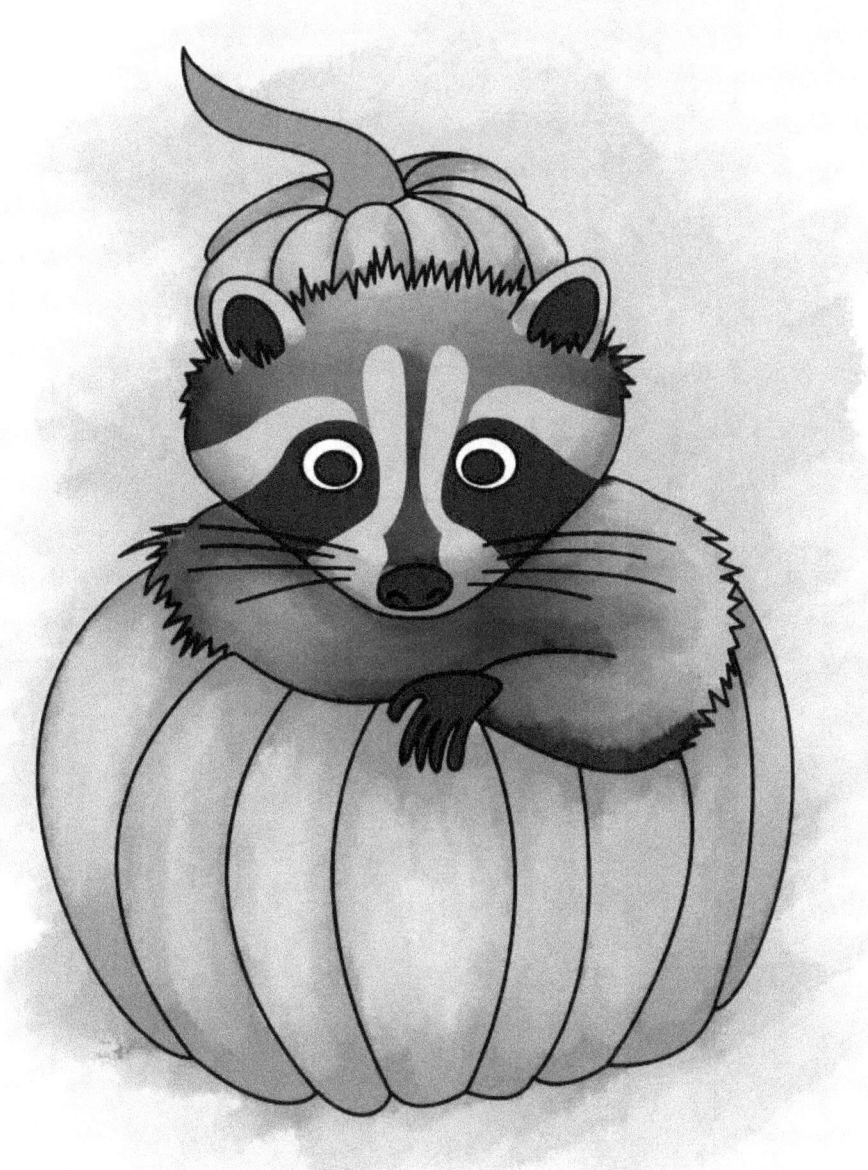

12) Colored version.

How to draw Racoon7

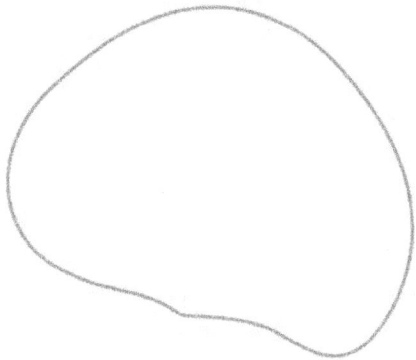

1) Draw a head just to the right of the center of the sheet.

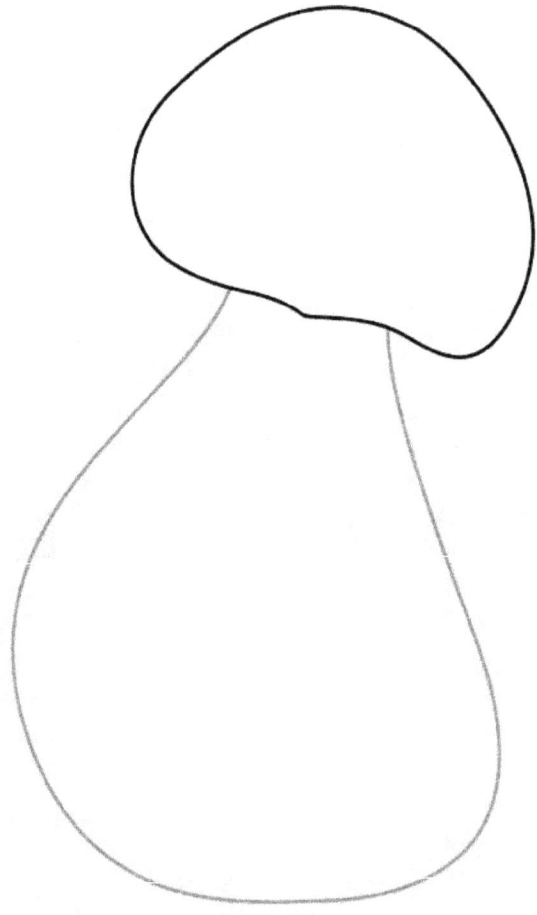

2) Add a drop-shaped body below.

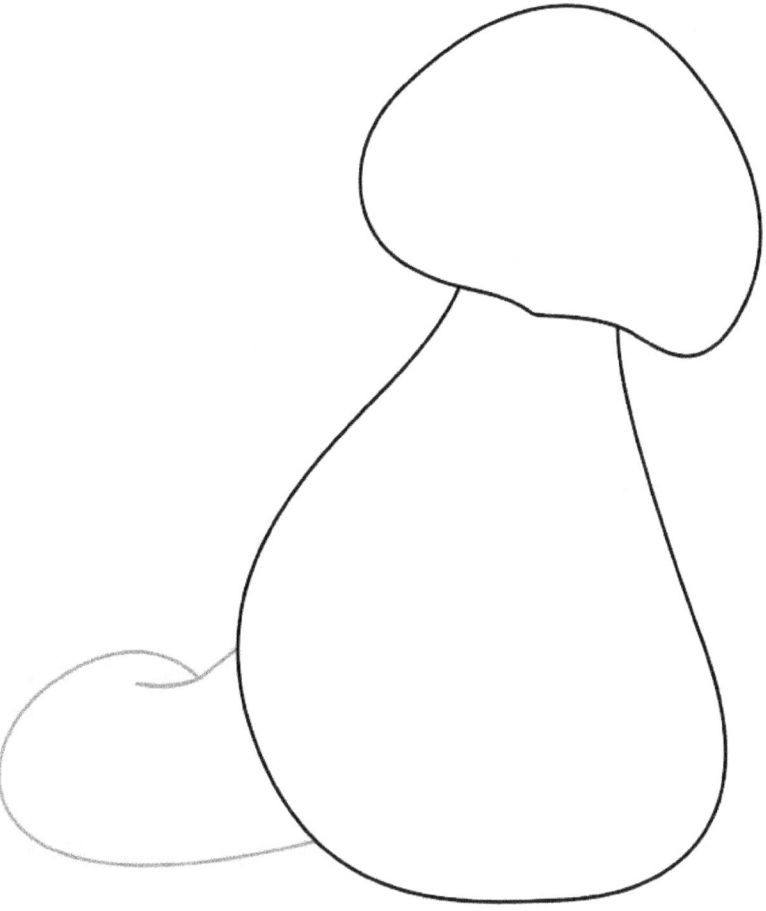

3) Draw the tail to the left, as shown in the example.

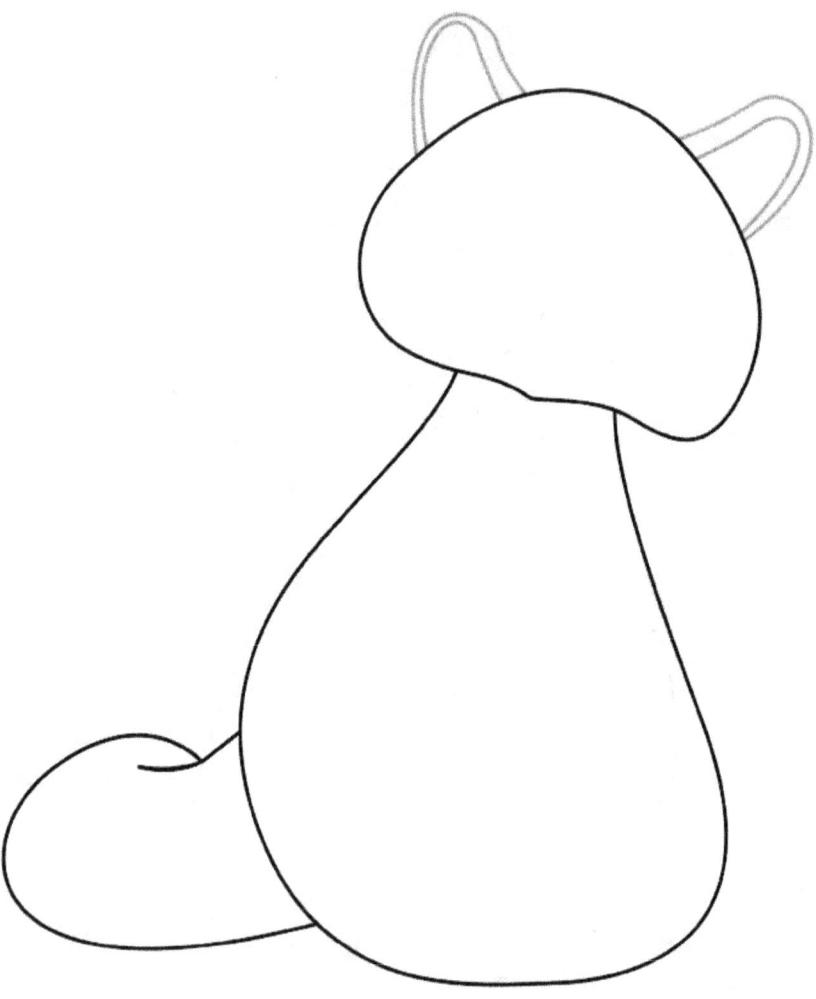

4) Draw two ears on the head.

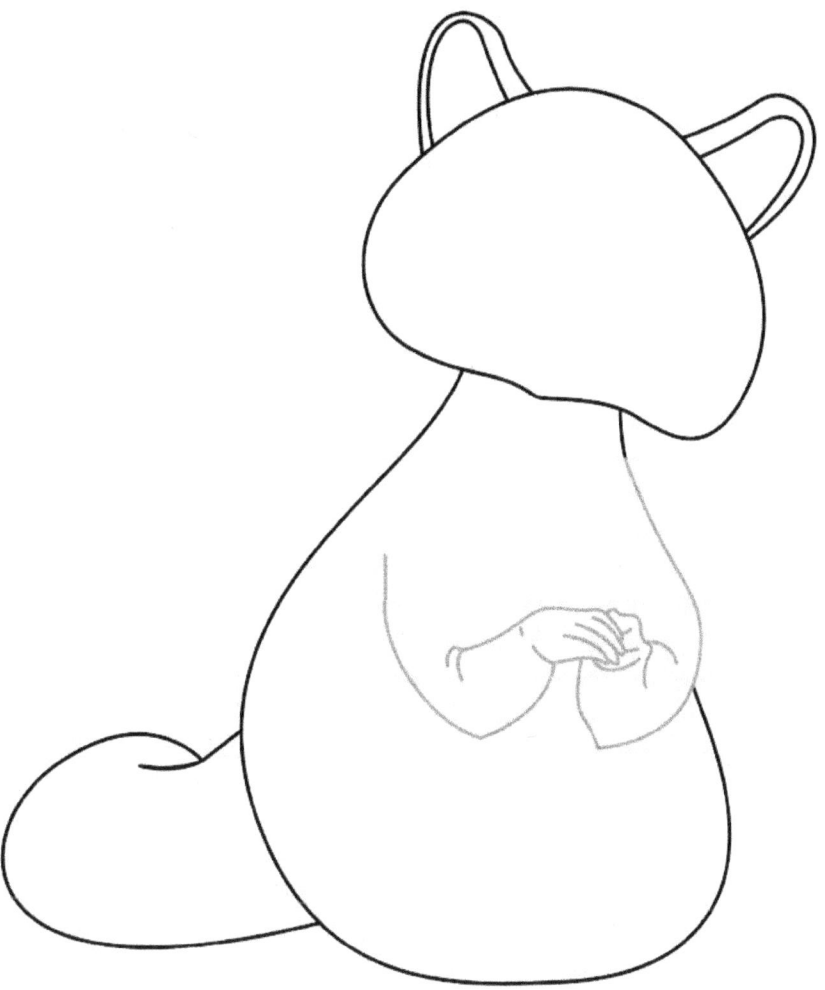

5) Draw bent front paws, folded on the chest.

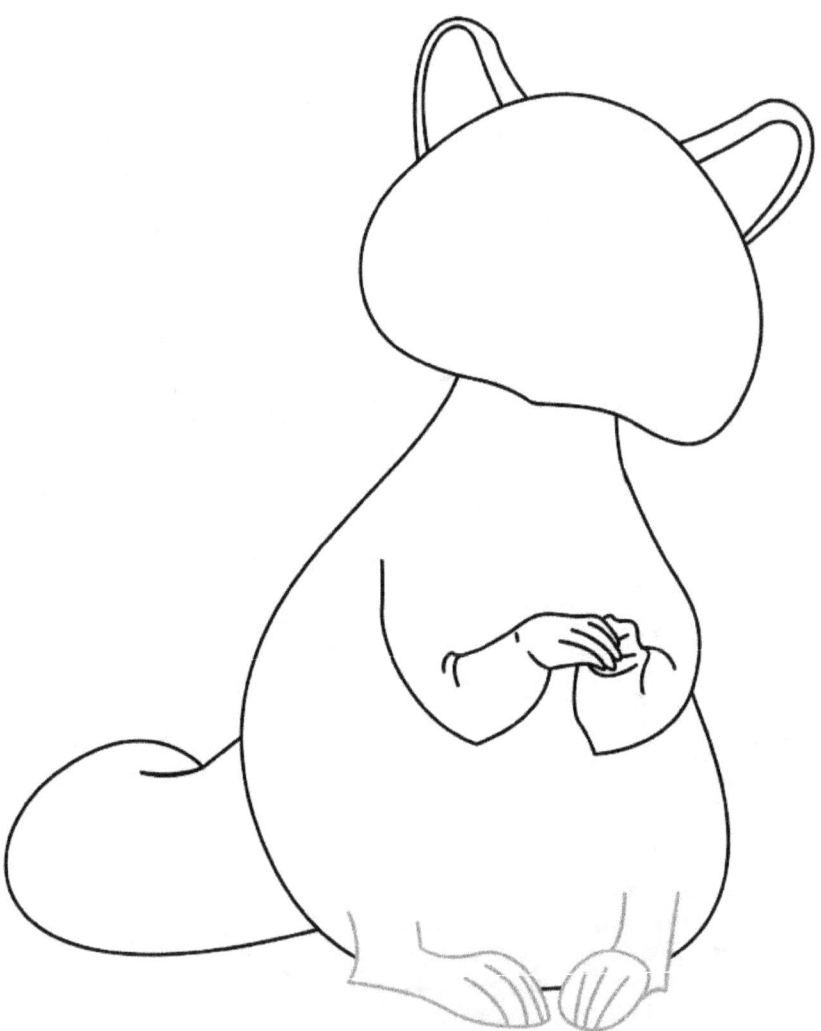

6) Draw hind legs, be close to the original.

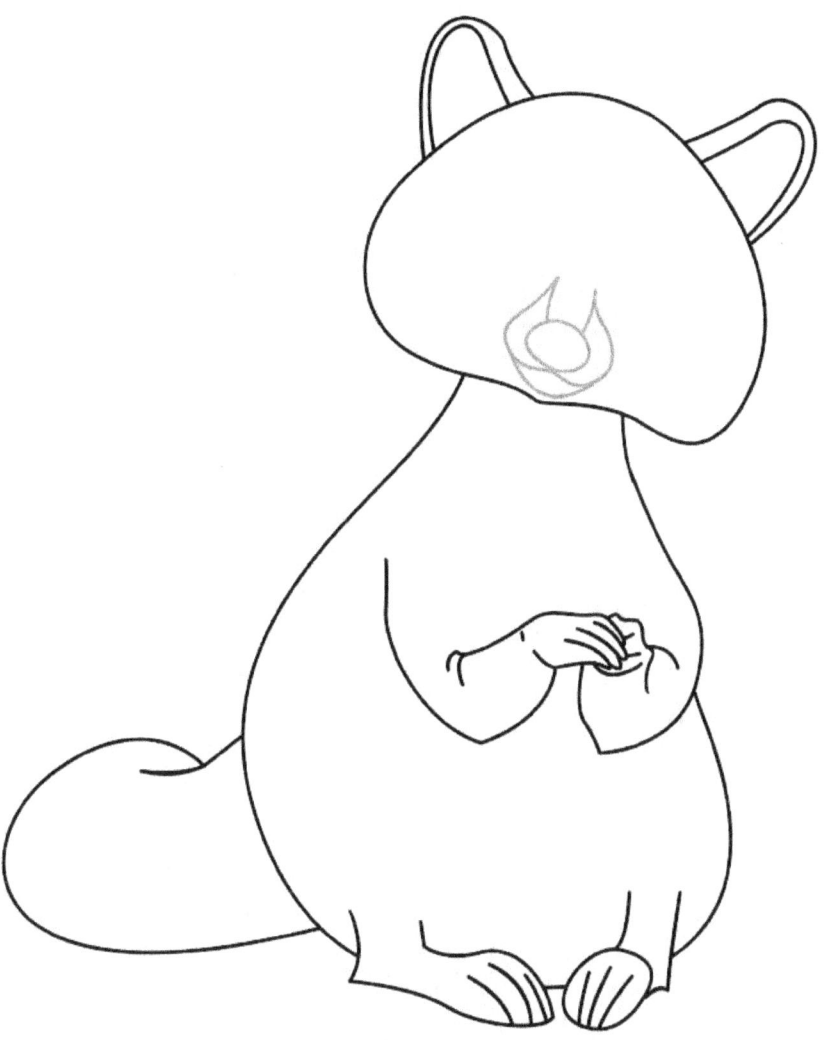

7) Draw a nose and mouth.

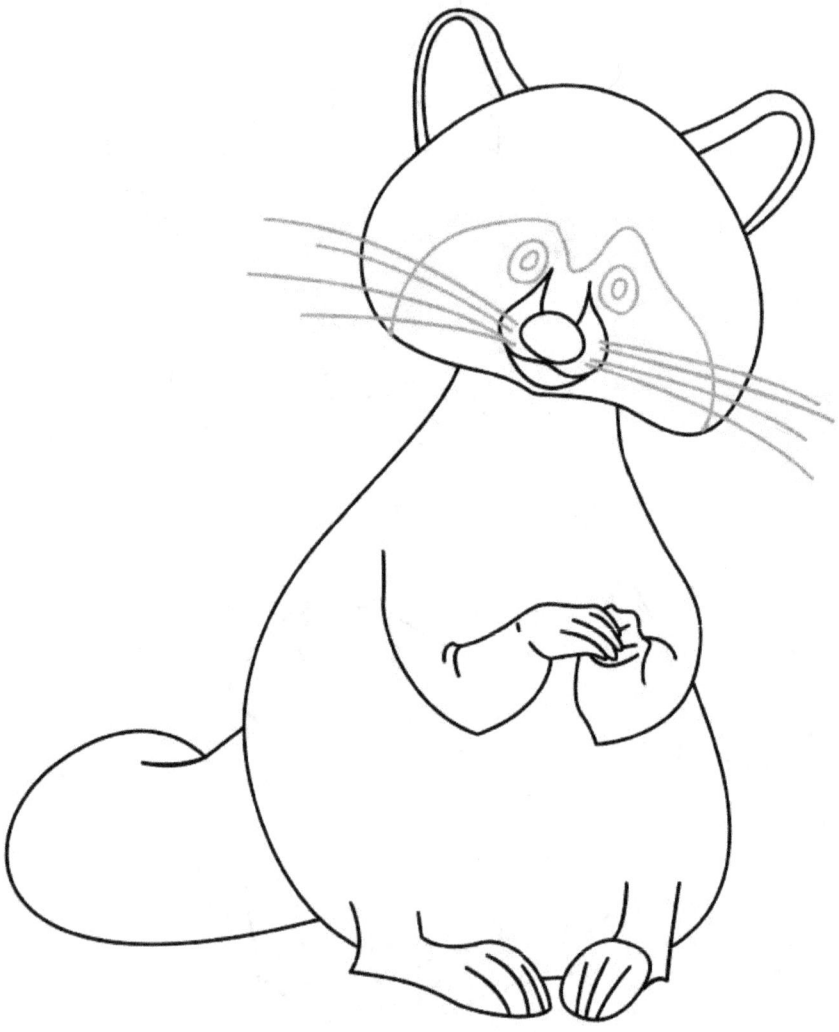

8) Draw small eyes, antennae and a line on the face around the
eyebrows.

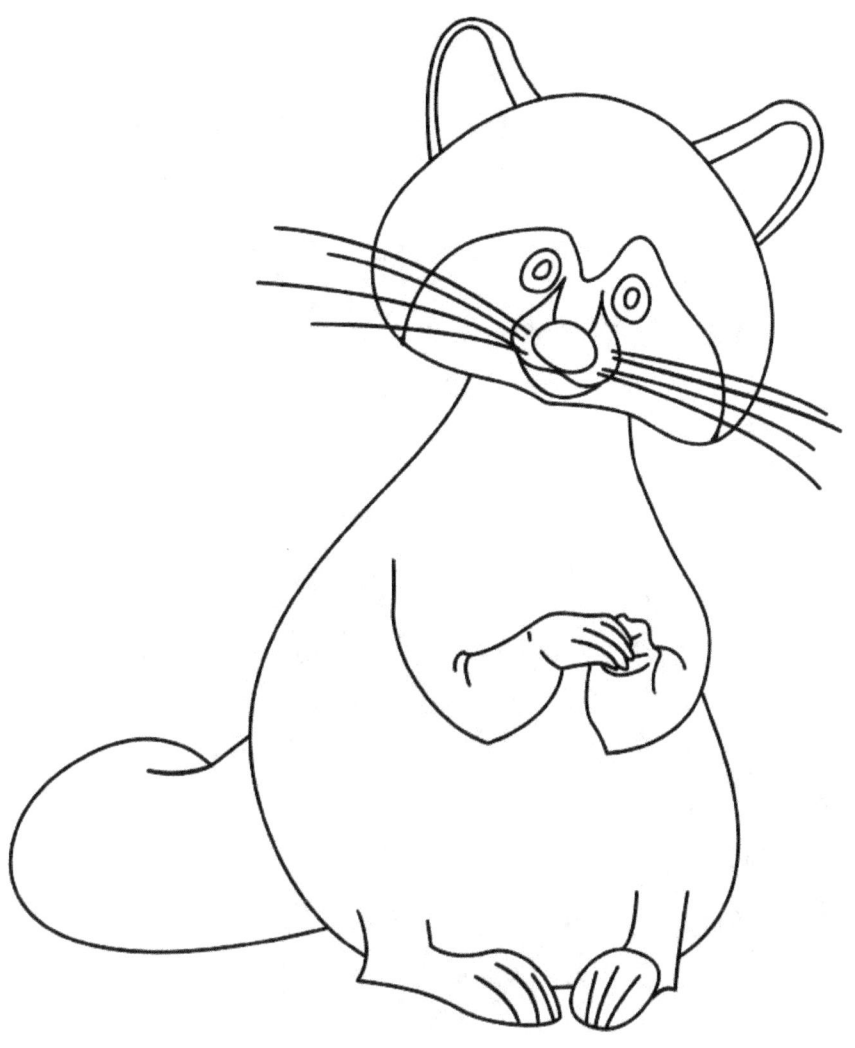

9) Done, let's start coloring!

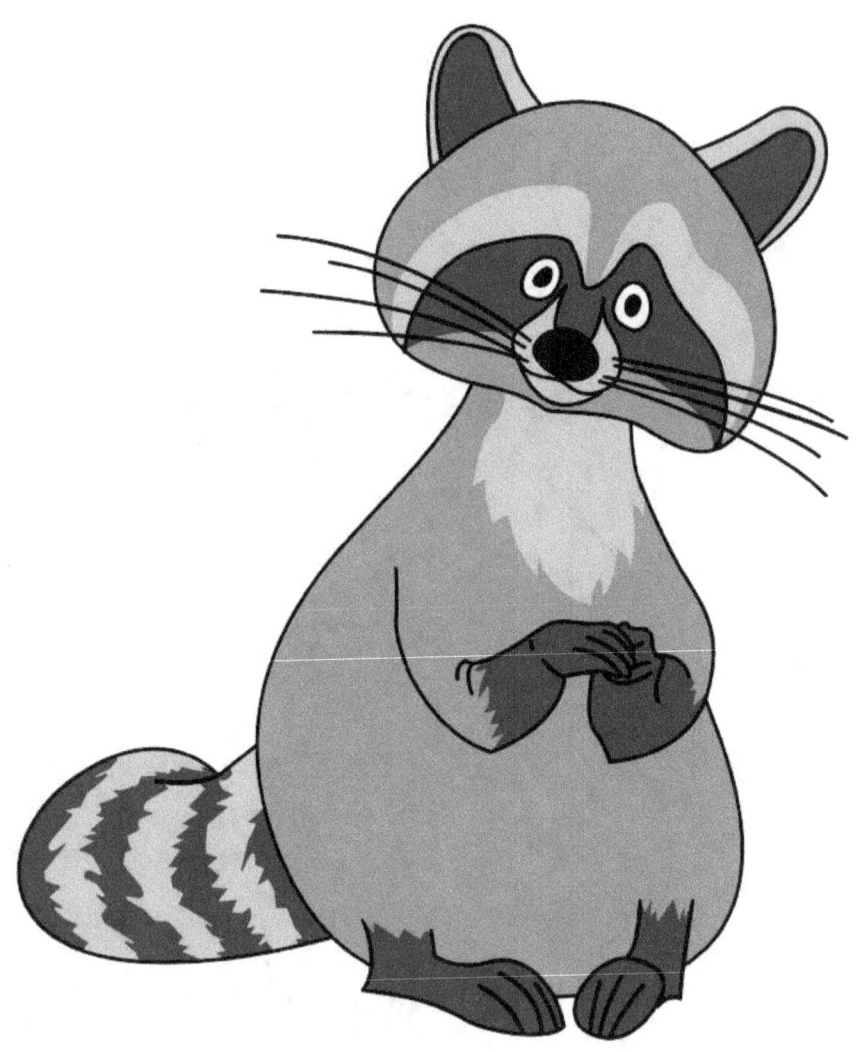

10) Color picture using grey and black for fur.

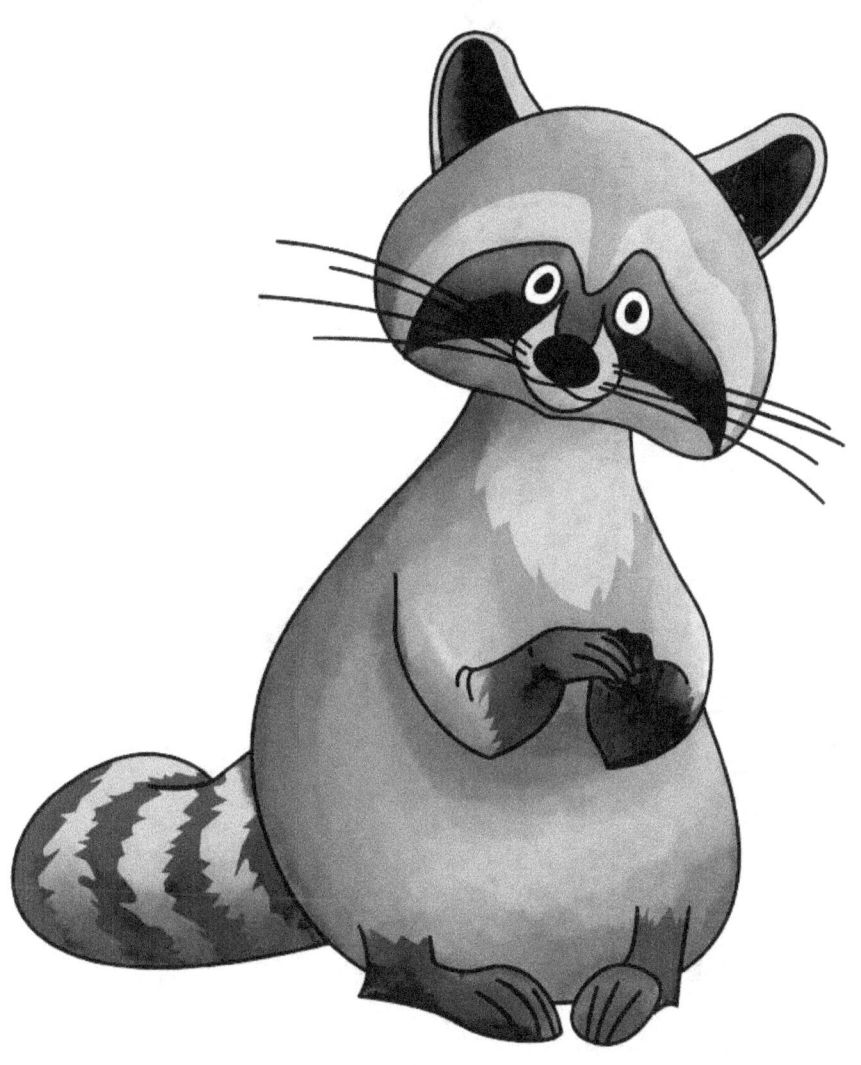

11) Add some shadows and highlights to add volume.

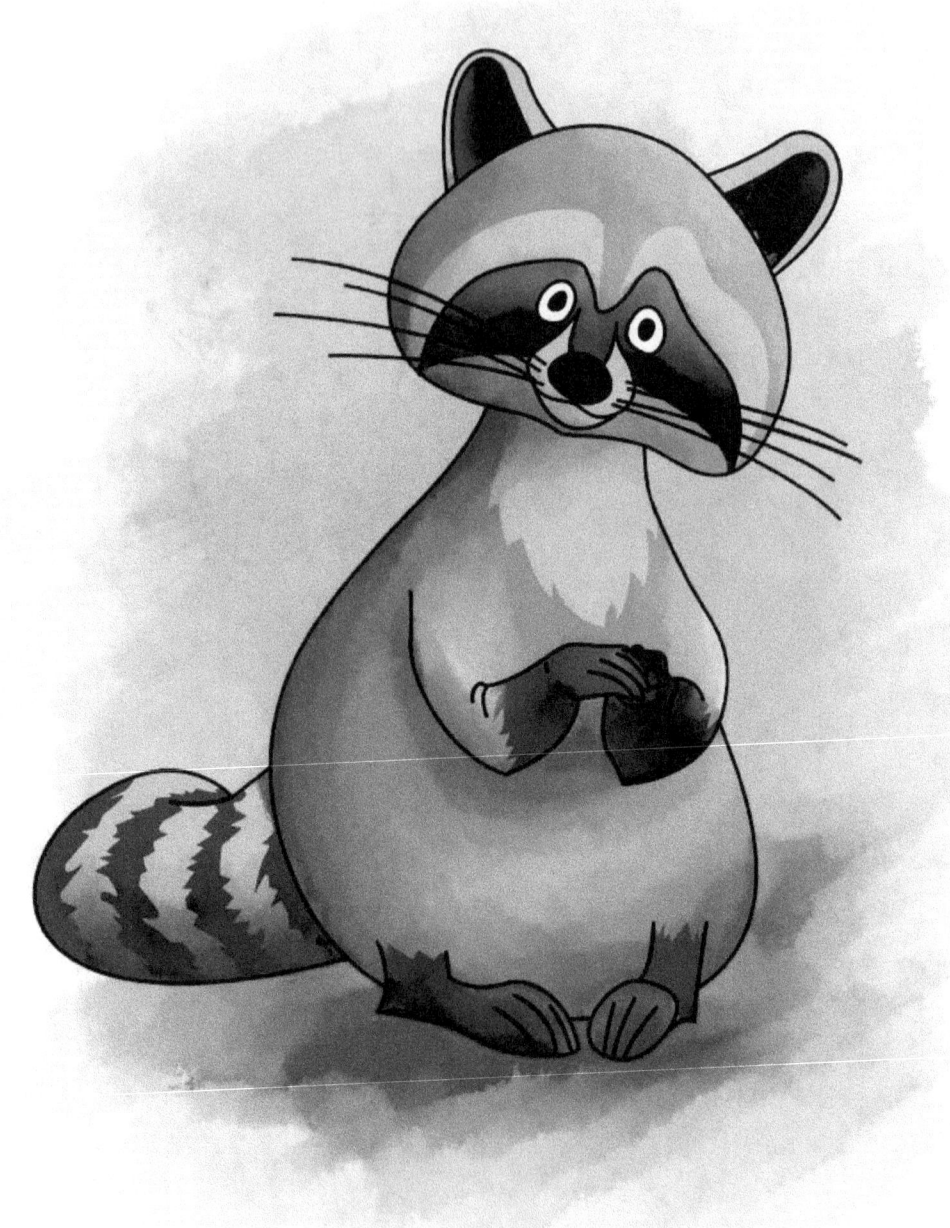

12) Colored version.

www.ingramcontent.com/pod-product-compliance
Lightning Source LLC
Chambersburg PA
CBHW081109290526
45795CB00006B/2057